The
Subtlest Battle

The
Subtlest Battle
Islam in Soviet Tajikistan

Muriel Atkin

FOREIGN POLICY RESEARCH INSTITUTE
Philadelphia
1989

Library of Congress Cataloging-in-Publication Data

Atkin, Muriel.
  The subtlest battle : Islam in Soviet Tajikistan / Muriel Atkin.
      p.   cm. — (The Philadelphia papers)
  ISBN 0-910191-09-3
  1. Islam—Tajik S.S.R.   2. Islam and politics—Tajik S.S.R.
  3. Tajik S.S.R.—Politics and government. I. Title. II. Series.
  BP63.T35A87   1989
  297'.0958'6—dc19   88-39067
                                                                CIP

Foreign Policy Research Institute
3615 Chestnut Street
Philadelphia, Pa. 19104

Contents

Foreword

In the pages that follow, Dr. Muriel Atkin provides a careful, scholarly, and important case-study of Islam in the Soviet Union. This essay on Tajikistan exemplifies the kind of calm, balanced analysis we so badly need, for the study of Soviet Islam and related subjects has been caught in the passions of the Iranian Revolution and the Soviet invasion of Afghanistan.

Three basic images of motivation have emerged in the West to account for the Soviet attitude toward the Iranian Revolution and the Soviet invasion of Afghanistan: the imperial, the opportunistic, and the defensive. Each school of interpretation has to deal with the question of Islam.

The imperial school sees the Soviet Union as an implacable and confident expansionist power; for it, the significance of Islam lies in its weakness, for it is deemed insufficient as a binding force to contain Soviet expansion toward the shores of the Indian Ocean.

The opportunistic school sees Soviet aggression as a more or less ad hoc and cautious response to targets of opportunity; here, Islam is typically seen as one of many factors that Soviet leaders must consider in their computations of a regional correlation of forces. But Islam, whether within or without Soviet borders, is not a decisive force. Thus, even if the Soviets knew that the invasion of Afghanistan would harm Soviet-Iranian relations and lead to riots in Kazakhstan, such costs were accepted and did not deter them.

The defensive school holds that the Soviet Union is a frail, slightly paranoid, and extremely cautious power; here the significance of Islam is critical. The argument that the Soviet military campaign in Afghanistan was defensively motivated invariably turns on supposed Soviet fears that the *mujahidin* in Afghanistan and the force of the Iranian Revolution would somehow infest Muslims in Soviet Central Asia, loosening and perhaps even jeopardizing Soviet control. Demographic trends within the Soviet Union show a much faster rise in Muslim populations; this has important implications for the Soviet labor and military manpower pools, and is seen as magnifying Russian fears.

These schools of interpretation hold many temptations for Western policy: the chimera of ending the U.S.-Soviet struggle by ending, in effect, the Soviet Union; the lure of assuming a benign decrepitude within Soviet society that allows us an option of unilateral disengagement; and the illusion of a secure refuge for the development of Western strategy abetted by false certainties about Soviet imperial ambitions reaching inexorably toward the "warm waters" of the Indian Ocean.

Before such speculations can be intelligently discussed, much more needs to be known about the possible future Achilles' heel of the USSR, the Muslim peoples of Central Asia. Despite many obstacles, careful scholars have been at work studying this subject.

The history of Soviet struggles against earlier generations of Muslim warriors, the Soviet attitude toward Islam, and recent Soviet policies have been analyzed. No one can now claim excusable ignorance about Tajikistan. Muriel Atkin carefully leads the reader through the nuances of Islamic life there as it abuts the power of the Soviet state.

Her topic is particularly relevant to many policy debates. Because Tajiks speak a Persian dialect instead of a Turkic one, they are arguably the Soviet Muslim group most likely to be infected by passions emanating from Iran. Yet, as Dr. Atkin shows, there is little evidence of any such contagion. This does not mean that the Soviet system has once and for all conquered Islam in Central Asia as a political force. Subtle and fluid accommodations have evolved between the Tajiks and the Soviet state; each side seems to sense where the boundaries of propriety lie. Both sides are constrained by the conventions of social control and communal prerogatives. Though disruptable in extreme circumstances, and contestable at the margin, the present modus operandi appears a good deal more stable than the third, defensive, school alleges.

I commend the study within these covers to experts and generalists, to the impassioned and the dispassionate. It is an edifying and enlightening work of scholarship.

Adam M. Garfinkle
Editor
The Philadelphia Papers

Introduction

In recent years [in Tajikistan], the clergy became active; they preach among the backward part of the population "theories" alien to our ideology, spread every tall tale, deflect weak-souled people from the true path .... According to incomplete data, just in the mountain and high mountain districts of Tajikistan in the past two years about one hundred mosques and many "holy places" were opened.[1]

The upsurge in Islamic political activism since the late 1970s has stimulated increased Western interest in the attitudes of the Soviet Union's large Muslim population. Some observers contend that Islam poses an increasing threat to the stability of the Soviet regime. According to this interpretation, the Islamic Revolution in Iran and the war of the Afghan *mujahidin* have encouraged restiveness among Soviet Muslims. But it is by no means certain that Islam poses an unmanageable problem for the Soviet leadership. The above epigraph, reflecting the distress of the Soviet authorities over the strength of Islam within the country, dates not from the 1980s but from 1963. It reminds us that, in attempting to gauge the strength of Islam as a dissident force in the Soviet Union, we must not confuse the phenomenon itself with either our own recently heightened interest in Soviet Islam or a similar, though more apprehensive, interest on the part of the Soviet authorities.

A significant proportion of Soviet citizens of Muslim ancestry probably still consider themselves Muslims, either in a diffuse cultural sense or as practicing believers. But, unfortunately, there is no reliable evidence to indicate how many Soviet citizens of Muslim ancestry do still consider themselves Muslims and, if so, in what sense they employ the term.[2] Soviet accounts, whether scholarly, journalistic, or propagandistic, reveal extensive and varied observance of Islam in the contemporary Soviet Union. From the tone of the discussion, it is clear that the authorities consider Islamic practice and identification strong enough to be a problem; it is, from officialdom's perspective, an obstacle to molding the "correct socialist outlook."

---

[1] G. Kalandarov, "Rasplata za bespechnost'," *Pravda*, May 27, 1963.

[2] For the sake of brevity, the term "Soviet Muslims" will be used for all the traditionally Muslim peoples of the Soviet Union, even though we have no way of knowing how many of them are still believers.

1

Soviet Muslims are believed to number between 45 million and 55 million, depending on how one interprets the 1979 census data and calculates population growth since. By comparison, an estimate from the early 1970s put the number of Russian Orthodox believers in the Soviet Union at 40 to 50 million.[3] The total Soviet population, according to the 1979 census, was more than 262 million, estimated to have risen to nearly 280 million by 1986. The census does not include information on religious beliefs. This number of Muslim citizens makes the Soviet Union the fifth largest Muslim country in the world (after Indonesia, Pakistan, Bangladesh, and India). The Soviet Union has slightly more Muslims than the most populous Muslim countries of the Middle East — Egypt, Turkey, and Iran.

Soviet Muslims are a diverse group. They speak many languages, most of which belong to the Turkic, Iranian, and Caucasian families. They live in a variety of geographic regions, but are concentrated in the river valleys of Central Asia, the Kazakh and Turkmen steppes, Transcaucasia, the high mountains of the Caucasus and the Pamirs, and the Volga region. A large majority of Soviet Muslims are Sunnis, although a Shi'i minority, mostly Azerbaijanis, exists. The ancestors of today's Soviet Muslims converted to Islam at different times over approximately a millennium, (from the seventh century to the eighteenth). These diverse peoples traditionally led separate, distinct ways of life; their historical experiences and cultural heritages differ widely from each other.

Although there is a traditionally respected principle that every Muslim is part of a single community of believers, the *umma*, this has meant far less in practice than in principle. The history of the Muslims in what is now the Soviet Union tells many tales of war and lesser animosities among dynastic states, tribes, peoples, and ambitious conquerors. Even in a situation conducive to unity — the widespread opposition among Central Asian Muslims to the forcible, often brutal, establishment of Soviet rule there during the civil war — the Basmachi movement, from 1918 intermittently until the mid-1930s, was divided by groups that failed to cooperate and occasionally even fought one another.[4]

The Western study of contemporary Soviet Islam has advanced to the point that we need to look not only collectively at all the Soviet Muslims but also at a greater range of specific groups. Some important Western writing about Islam in the Soviet Union today focuses on Sufism, which may be not only the most vital form of the religion in the Soviet Union but also, according to some, the most politically

---

[3] J. B. Dunlop, *The Faces of Contemporary Russian Nationalism* (Princeton: Princeton University Press, 1983), p. 169.

[4] R. Pipes, *The Formation of the Soviet Union*, rev. ed. (Cambridge, Mass.: Harvard University Press, 1964), pp. 178, 257.

militant. The main sources of information used in such studies pertain to the various peoples of the north and northeastern Caucasus and the Turkmens of Central Asia. That is not surprising, given that the Soviet discussion of Sufism, on which foreign scholars necessarily must rely to a considerable degree, also gives more attention to these peoples than to others.

Yet these most-studied peoples constitute but a small fraction of the total of Soviet Muslims and may not be representative. The total population of the north and northeastern Caucasus and Turkmenistan (regardless of religion or nationality) amounted to about 5 million as of the 1979 census, compared with a total number of about 45 million Soviet Muslims at that time. Moreover, these most-studied peoples have often had less-than-cordial relations with other Muslims, whether on religious or other grounds. The modern history of the Turkmens has been marked by repeated conflicts with their Uzbek neighbors in the khanates of Khiva and Bukhara (as well as with Iran). One veteran Western observer of Soviet Islam considers Islam as practiced in the Caucasus, with its inward focus and self-isolation, to be profoundly different in spirit from Islam as practiced in Central Asia.[5]

This study assesses the status of Islam in one Soviet republic, Tajikistan,[6] which shares a 644-mile border with Afghanistan (slightly less than half the entire Soviet-Afghan border). Tajik, a dialect of Persian, provides a linguistic link to Iran and Afghanistan (where dialects of Persian are the native language of several million inhabitants and the lingua franca for most of the rest). The Tajiks differentiate sharply between themselves and their Turkic-speaking neighbors. The Tajik intelligentsia's officially endorsed history of their people portrays Tajiks as contributors and heirs to 2,500 years of high Iranian civilization, a heritage shared with Afghanistan and Iran.[7]

[5] H. Carrère d'Encausse, *L'Empire éclaté* (Paris: Flammarion, 1978), p. 242.

[6] Tajikistani personal and place names will be transliterated from the Tajik rather than through the intermediary of Russian, unless they are part of a title or a byline in a Russian-language source. Direct transliteration produces fewer clumsy spellings and avoids distortions of meaning. For example, Tajik uses a single letter for the sound represented in English by "j"; Russian has no equivalent symbol and must resort to the bulkier "dzh." The distortions of Russian transliteration can also convert a word that conveys meaning in its own right into one that does not. The same Tajik root, "panj" (which means "five"), is transliterated by Russian in two different ways in two different place names: "Piandzh" (for the river forming the border with Afghanistan and the adjoining district of Tajikistan) and "Pendzhikent" (a city near the Tajikistan-Uzbekistan border). The Russian equivalent will accompany the first mention of a personal or place name. Diacritical marks have been omitted to avoid clutter. This transliteration system serves as a reminder that Tajiks, like many minorities in many countries, sometimes have two names, one within their own community and another in the dominant society.

[7] The most important contemporary Soviet interpretation of Tajik history — by B. Gh. Ghafurov (B. G. Gafurov, 1908-1977), former head of the Communist Party of Tajikistan, the republic's Academy of Sciences, and the Institute of Oriental Studies of the All-Union Academy of Sciences in Moscow — treats the history of the Tajiks as covering what is now Tajikistan as well as other parts of southern Central Asia, Iran, and Afghanistan. See B. Gh. Ghafurov, *Tojikon*, rev. ed. (Dushanbe: Irfon, 1983), vol. 1.

Most Muslims in Tajikistan are Sunni, as elsewhere in Central Asia and Afghanistan. A Shi'i minority (composed of Ismailis, estimated some years ago to number about 100,000) lives primarily in the high Pamir Mountains. They are not Tajiks, but belong to a number of smaller ethnic groups that speak other Iranian languages.

The population of Tajikistan numbered 4.5 million in early 1985. No breakdown of the ethnic composition is available for this update of the 1979 census, but in 1979 Tajiks constituted almost 60 percent of the republic's population, and Uzbeks, the second largest nationality, about 23 percent. Tajikistan has the highest rate of natural population increase, 3.01 percent, of all Soviet republics.[8] This means that it is common for women to make the rearing of many children a central part of their lives, and also that much of the population is young. These factors are relevant to the status and future of Islam in the region.

To ascertain whether Islam is a politically dissident force in Tajikistan and whether Islamic political activism in Iran and Afghanistan has encouraged such dissent, we must first look at how Islam influences the lives of the republic's inhabitants. Subsequent chapters deal with the domestic and external factors that encourage identification with Islam and with the controls employed by the Soviet system.

[8] *Naselenie SSSR* (Moscow: Politizdat, 1983), p. 189; Ministerstvo Vysshego i srednego spetsial'nogo obrazovaniia SSSR, *Naselenie SSSR segodnia*, vol. 38 (Moscow: Finansy i Statistika, 1982), pp. 39-40, table 2.

Tajikistan
and the Islamic Life

After some seventy years of communist rule and the systematic campaign against religion that has accompanied it, Soviet Islam is much more than a vestige of a pre-revolutionary social order. It continues to influence the lives of many, both as an indelible component of national culture and as a system of belief. Formal observances and popular customs widespread in the Muslim world in general also survive among Soviet Muslims. While Islam has been adapted to the conditions of Soviet life, it has not become a denatured hybrid. Islam in the Soviet Union is diverse both in its followers' adherence to tradition and in their adaptation to the requirements of Soviet society.

Belief

The Number of Believing Muslims. The standard Soviet assessment of the extent to which Islam is still practiced within Soviet borders is the formulaic assertion that most people of Muslim background have become atheists, but that believers who are neither firm in their belief nor strictly observant remain numerous. According to this formulation, the more time passes, the more the science of dialectical materialism replaces obscurantist religion.[1] Konstantin Chernenko's address to the June 15, 1983, Plenum of the Central Committee of the Communist Party of the Soviet Union (CPSU) noted that a considerable part of the population remains under religious influence (not specifically Islamic) and called for increased countermeasures.[2] On the local level, similar statements are made regarding the persistence of Islam in Tajikistan.[3]

[1] Typical of numerous statements to this effect are *Islam v SSSR* (Moscow: Mysl', 1983), pp. 66, 68; and M. Khalmukhamedov, "O chem govoriat musul'manskie propovedniki," *Nauka i religiia*, 1969, no. 6, p. 57.

[2] "Aktual'nye voprosy ideologicheskoi, massovo-politicheskoi raboty partii," *Agitator Tadzhikistana*, 1983, no. 14 (July), p. 24.

[3] N. Boimurodov, "Sotsializmi mutaraqqi va ozodii vijdon," *Kommunisti Tojikiston*, 1983, no. 12 (December), p. 74; M. Khojaev and Gh. Nu'monov, "Propagandai ateistiro ta"sirbakhsh menamoem," *Kommunisti Tojikiston*, 1982, no. 10 (October), p. 77.

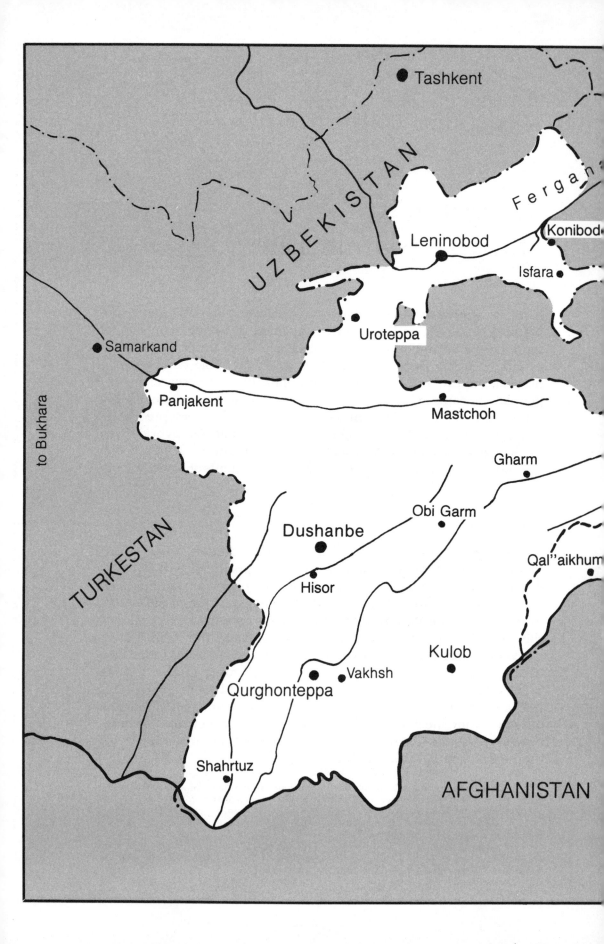

TAJIKISTAN

Soviet writings of a more scholarly, less political nature recognize Islam's still quite powerful influence in the USSR. One of the foremost specialists on Central Asia, T. S. Saidbaev, contends that the Islamic regions of the Soviet Union are the least secularized parts of the country. He also considers the persistence of Islam different from the persistence of other religions because, in the case of Islam, belief is not confined to women and the elderly.[4] A sociological study of religion in Tajikistan reportedly concludes that the level of religious belief there "remains high" and exerts a powerful "emotional influence."[5] These assertions provide only a vague estimate of the level of Islamic belief. As James Critchlow, an American expert on Uzbekistan, has noted, "No one, including the Soviet government and the local clergy, knows how many of the USSR's Muslim millions are true believers, or how widely they practice their religion."[6]

The Social Composition of the Muslim Community. Many Soviet discussions of Islam in Tajikistan and elsewhere emphasize that a majority of believers are elderly. The same is said of Russian Orthodox believers. This view serves to comfort Soviet officialdom, for it permits them to believe that most practicing Muslims acquired their beliefs early in the Soviet era and are those people least affected by the subsequent transformation of society. It also encourages the hope that the passage of time will soon remove these believers.[7]

But time may increase the problem rather than solve it. There are indications that on retirement some people who had not previously appeared to be observant Muslims begin to display an active interest in Islam. The timing of this change suggests that advancing age and release from the requirements of the workplace encourage greater attention to spiritual values; also, those who are retired no longer need fear damaging their careers by being known as believers.

The only recent literary work of note in the Tajik language that deals with the persistence of Islam focuses precisely on this issue. The play, *Dar Chorsu* (At the crossroads), by Nur Tabarov, has been well received by Tajikistani authorities, including the party first secretary, Q. M. Mahkamov (K. M. Makhkamov), who singled it out for

---

[4] T. S. Saidbaev, *Islam i obshchestvo*, 2nd ed., (Moscow: Nauka. Glavnaia redaktsiia Vostochnoi literatury, 1984), pp. 5, 202; all citations will be to this edition unless otherwise noted.

[5] S. Iu. Dadabaeva, "Konkretno-sotsiologicheskie issledovaniia v praktike ateisticheskoi raboty," Akademiia obshchestvennykh nauk TsK KPSS, Institut nauchnogo ateizma, *Voprosy Nauchnogo Ateizma*, vol. 31: *Sovremennyi islam i problemy ateisticheskogo vospitaniia* (Moscow: Mysl', 1983), pp. 253, 258; "Vazhnaia chast' ideologicheskoi raboty," *Agitator Tadzhikistana*, 1980, no. 13 (July), p. 2.

[6] J. Critchlow, "Minarets and Marx," *The Washington Quarterly*, Spring 1980, p. 50.

[7] Typical of this view are Ch. Komilov, "Propagandai ateisti va rohhoi behtar kardani on," *Kommunisti Tojikiston*, 1983, no. 6 (June), p. 75; and M. Jabborova, "Ba"ze problemahoi tarbiyai ateistii javonon," *Kommunisti Tojikiston*, 1985, no. 1 (January), p. 88.

praise.[8] This presumably indicates officialdom's perception that the message is correct and that it describes a significant manifestation of Islamic observance.

The most striking feature of the play's story is that the retirees who are now particularly zealous Muslims were all Communist party members who had occupied local positions of some responsibility within the Soviet system.[9] This seems to parallel aspects of real life in Tajikistan. A recent newspaper article described supposedly atheist party members who became practicing Muslims after retirement. The article tells the story of one Emomali Rabiev, a former schoolteacher and party member. On retirement, he not only became observant but also became a self-styled mullah, a teacher of religious dogma.[10]

Such stories about retirees show that the degree of Islamic belief among men of pre-retirement age may be higher than can readily be discerned. (The stories always deal with men, probably because relatively few Muslim women in Tajikistan have careers that could be jeopardized by being known as an observant Muslim; most are either homemakers or work in low-level agricultural jobs.) Men who become overt believers in old age may have observed the rites of their faith covertly all along, or at least remembered them from childhood. For example, a party member employed as a *sovkhoz* director in the postwar era, Nuriddin Saidov, built over many years a reputation as a responsible official. At the same time, he trained one of his sons to become a mullah. According to a hostile account, he also taught his son how to lead a double life. When the elder Saidov retired, he turned in his party card voluntarily and became a mullah.[11]

Children, who constitute nearly half the population in Tajikistan,[12] are also counted among the practicing Muslims. Although it is impossible to discern exactly how many are believers, whatever the number, it is too high to suit the Soviet authorities. As usual, they argue that only a minority of young people are believers and that observance of Islam is strongest in rural areas, where adults are also more likely to be observant; in fact, it also occurs in the cities. The Tenth Plenum of the Central Committee of the Communist Party of Tajikistan (which was held specifically to apply to Tajikistan the results of the June 1983 Plenum of the Central Committee of the

[8] TadzhikTA, "Utverzhdaia pravdu zhizni," *Kommunist Tadzhikistana*, March 30, 1986, p.2 (Mahkamov's speech to the Ninth Congress of the Tajikistan Writers' Union).

[9] Q. Vose", "'Dar chorsu'-i andeshaho," *Gazetai muallimon*, June 11, 1985, p. 3; S. Mirzoev, "Perekrestok," *Komsomolets Tadzhikistana*, March 27, 1985, p. 4.

[10] N. Safarov, "Tarbiyai ateisti — kori purmas"ul," *Tojikistoni Soveti*, June 11, 1986, p. 2.

[11] A. Sanginov, "Ashki nadomat," *Tojikistoni Soveti*, February 14, 1987, p. 4.

[12] T. I. Fedorova, *Goroda Tadzhikistana i problemy rosta i razvitiia.* (Dushanbe: Irfon, 1981), p.39.

CPSU) called for increased atheist propaganda, especially among the young.[13]

Religious affiliation persists among some of Tajikistan's most educated students. A survey conducted between 1973 and 1982 at the Polytechnic Institute in Dushanbe (the capital of Tajikistan) reportedly indicated that 78 percent of the students considered themselves atheists. Under the circumstances, that figure is not impressively high. Young people being trained for some of the more promising kinds of careers — such as skilled technical jobs — would have good reason to answer positively when asked whether they were atheists. There is no way to verify whether the figure quoted is accurate. The report says nothing about the nationality and religious background of those surveyed.[14] The meaning of that 78 percent figure is reduced still further when the article states that many students in Tajikistan's institutions of higher education believe in "superstitions"; a close look shows that many of these superstitions are elements of folk Islam, including belief in the efficacy of the evil eye, *jinns*, and fortune telling.[15] Islamic observance by young Tajikistanis is manifested through attending prayers in mosques, wearing new clothes in honor of religious holidays, being married according to traditional Islamic rites, obtaining instruction from unofficial mullahs, and fasting during Ramadan. Some students openly resist the school's efforts to convert them to atheism.[16]

Soviet sources routinely describe Tajik women as highly religious, far more so than the men — similar to the assertions about Soviet Muslim women in general.[17] While this may indeed be the

---

[13] Jabborova, "Ba"ze problemahoi," p. 88; Komilov, "Ba"ze sababhoi dindorii maktabiyon va rohhoi barham dodani onho," *Maktabi Soveti*, 1982, no. 11 (November), p. 12; N. Boimurodov, "Sotsializmi mutaraqqi," p. 75; "Jam"basti plenumi iyuni (soli 1983) KM KPSS," *Kommunisti Tojikiston*, 1983, no. 8 (August), p. 6; R. Tagaeva, "Doiti do serdtsa kazhdogo," *Agitator Tadzhikistana*, 1983, no. 16 (August), p.23; Dadabaeva, "Konkretno-sotsiologicheskie issledovaniia," p. 252; N. Safarov, "Tarbiyai ateisti," p. 2.

[14] This matters because Tajikistan's Tajiks and Uzbeks are predominantly rural and tend not to go to the big cities to complete their education, while Russians made up a majority of Dushanbe's population as of the 1970 census, the last date for which data on the city's ethnic composition were released. See Sh. Shoismatulloev, "Chorsui zindagi," *Adabiyot va san"at*, July 26, 1984, p. 3; R. Bobojonov, "Islohoti maktab va vazifaho oid ba kasbintikhobkununi khonandagon," *Maktabi Soveti*, 1985, no. 4 (April), p. 4; Ia. R. Vinnikov, "Natsional'nye i etnograficheskie gruppy Srednei Azii po dannym etnicheskoi statistiki," *Etnicheskie protesessy u natsional'nykh grupp Srednei Azii i Kazakhstana* (Moscow: Nauka, 1980), p. 20.

[15] Jabborova, "Ba"ze problemahoi," pp. 87, 89.

[16] Dadabaeva, "Konkretno-sotsiologicheskie issledovaniia," p. 257; Komilov, "Ba"ze sababhoi dindorii," p. 12; Dadabaeva, "Sama saboi ne otomret," *Kommunist Tadzhikistana*, October 31, 1980, p. 2; T. Khurshedova, "Vospityvat' primerami iz zhizni," *Agitator Tadzhikistana*, 1985, no. 23 (December), p. 26; R. Madzhidov, "Znachenie kul'turnoi revoliutsii v preodolenii religioznykh perezhitkov," *Voprosy nauchnogo ateizma*, ed. M. R. Rakhimov (Dushanbe: Donish, 1966), p. 37; "Maktab va tarbiyai ateistii khonandagon," *Gazetai Muallimon*, January 17, 1984, p. 4.

[17] S. Ahmadov, "San"at va tashakkuli jahonbinii ilmii ateistii mehnatkashon," *Kommunisti Tojikiston*, 1983, no. 8 (August), p. 94; M. Khojaev and Gh. Nu"monov, "Propagandai ateistiro ta"sirbakhsh menamoem," *Kommunisti Tojikiston*, 1982, no. 10, (October), p. 77; *Islam v SSSR*,

case, it should be kept in mind that religiosity among working-age men may simply be more difficult to detect. Further, above the age of forty-five, women substantially outnumber men in Tajikistan.[18] One sociological survey conducted in Tajikistan reportedly found that 50.2 percent of the women questioned identified themselves as believers. Although the account does not say so, it implies that Islam was the only religion in question.[19] According to Soviet sources, the religious observances of women are associated with the practices of folk Islam, such as praying at shrines and seeking the help of occult practitioners.

Soviet sources treat Islam in Tajikistan as a predominantly rural phenomenon,[20] and there are indeed many believers in the country-side. But two considerations are pertinent here. Soviet writers are reluctant to describe Islam as strong in the cities, because cities are supposed to be in the forefront of society's advance and therefore are presumed to have rejected "outmoded" belief in religion. Second, Tajikistan's population was 66 percent rural in 1985,[21] and the proportion of village dwellers who are Muslims must be even higher, for the ethnic Russian population (slightly more than 10 percent) is heavily urban.

Some proportion of those people the Soviet authorities expect to take the lead in instilling communist values — party members and the intelligentsia — are themselves observant or at least tolerate religious observance by others.[22] For them, participation in the standard rites of Islam, like gatherings to break the Ramadan fast or the various life-cycle rituals, have social and emotional significance in addition to their more narrow spiritual import.[23]

The officially approved explanation downplays the degree of religiosity that this implies, asserting that these *intelligenty* do not believe in Islam as a religion, but practice various traditional life-cycle rites because they see them as national traditions.[24] Certainly, some Muslims who are making their way within the Soviet establishment may feel a strong cultural attachment to Islamic customs without believing in Islamic religious dogma; one can find a similar attachment among Christians and Jews in secular Western societies. However, some of Tajikistan's *intelligenty* may be religiously Muslim

pp. 77-78; R. Madzhidov, *Osobennosti formirovaniia ateisticheskogo mirovozzreniia zhensh-chin* (Dushanbe: Donish, 1977), pp. 42, 44.

[18] N. Khonaliev, "Aholi, zahiraho va istifodai onho," *Sadoi Sharq*, 1983, no.4, p. 68.

[19] Dadabaeva, "Konkretno-sotsiologicheskie issledovaniia," p. 254.

[20] R. Ahmedova, "Na osnove kompleksnogo podkhoda," *Agitator Tadzhikistana*, 1983, no. 23 (December), p. 17; R. Tagaeva, "Doiti do serdtsa kazhdogo," *Agitator Tadzhikistana*, 1983, no. 16 (August), p. 23.

[21] A. Sattorov, "Deha simoi shahr megirad," *Tojikistoni Soveti*, January 29, 1986, p.2.

[22] The term "intelligentsia" in Soviet usage has evolved to mean anyone in the arts or professions or possessing some higher education. Many are party members.

[23] Saidbaev, *Islam i obshchestvo*, pp. 227, 232-33.

[24] Dadabaeva, "Sama soboi ne otomret," p. 2; *Islam v SSSR*, p. 68; Saidbaev, *Islam i obshchestvo*, p. 219.

too. One indication that this is so is the complaint that the Soviet variety of modernizing Islam, which argues that Islamic social values harmonize with those of Marxism, has "deluded" some *intelligenty* into believing in Islamic teachings.[25]

Though all members of the Communist party are supposed to be atheists, some party members in Tajikistan are practicing Muslims. Martha Olcott believes it not unusual for Muslims in Central Asia to be party members, something that is most unusual for Christians anywhere in the Soviet Union.[26] Even in Dushanbe, where pressures to conform must be strongest, party members and others with some authority reportedly pray in clandestine mosques and listen to unofficial mullahs.[27] Some party members are said to engage in other Islamic practices, including making a pilgrimage to local holy places.[28] In recent years, party members have been faulted for insufficient efforts to curb religion and encourage atheism. The targets of criticism range from unnamed individuals to primary party organizations, *raion* (district)-level party committees, and the Tajikistan minister of culture.[29] This kind of charge is nothing new. In 1963, one of the highest-ranking members of the Communist Party of Tajikistan, N. Zaripov, a secretary of the party's Central Committee, was criticized by Moscow for blocking distribution of a film about the high level of Sufi activity in a particular village. Zaripov allegedly argued that there was no need for films that undermine the authority of the holy men.[30]

It is not clear exactly what price a party member pays if he is accused of being soft on Islam or of practicing Islam himself. Presumably, specific criticism of the type mentioned above, especially when made by a ranking official, does not bode well for one's standing. One *oblast'* (province)-level party secretary has made an ambiguous reference to religiously observant party members having been penalized by their organizations.[31]

The attitudes of teachers toward religion have evoked expressions of concern, not only because teachers mold the outlook of the young, but also because they are an important channel for extending the state's influence over the large rural population. Teachers are supposed to be models of correct Soviet behavior in their personal

---

[25] Boimurodov, "Sotsializmi mutaraqqi," p. 75.

[26] M. B. Olcott, "Soviet Islam and World Revolution," *World Politics*, July 1982 p. 495.

[27] TadzhikTA, "Pretvorim v zhizn' resheniia XXVII s"ezda KPSS!" *Kommunist Tadzhikistana*, April 20, 1986, p. 3.

[28] Tagaeva, "Doiti do serdtsa kazhdogo," p. 24; Sanginov, "Ashki nadomat," p.4. The regions involved are Kulob (Kuliab) and Qurghonteppa (Kurgan-Tiube) *oblast'* in southern Tajikistan.

[29] Tagaeva, "Doiti do serdtsa kazhdogo," p.24; TadzhikTA, "Pretvorim v zhizn'," p. 3; N. Safarov, "Tarbiyai ateisti," p. 2; Sanginov, "Ashki nadomat," p.4; V. Rabiev, "Idushchie v nikuda," *Kommunist Tadzhikistana*, February 12, 1987, p.3.

[30] V. Surkov, "Komandirovka v rai," *Izvestiia*, September 26, 1963.

[31] Tagaeva, "Doiti do serdtsa kazhdogo," p. 24.

lives. Tajikistani press complaints indicate that some teachers do just the opposite. Either they are not active advocates of atheism or they are actually practicing Muslims. Some teach classes on atheism poorly or not at all, or even thwart such instruction. Others observe Islamic practices, such as life-cycle rituals, fasting during Ramadan, or seeking a mullah's help in curing illness or obtaining sons.[32]

Observances and Attitudes

How Soviet Muslims practice their religion is especially difficult to ascertain because so much can be done in private. Islam is not only a body of spiritual teachings but is also a guide to the conduct of everyday life. Such mundane matters as eating and bathing are bound up with Islamic sensibilities and cannot be separated from them. Moreover, identification with the Islamic heritage does not require strict adherence to all the traditionally required observances, public or private, any more than it does for other adherents of other religions who live in a secular environment. Nonetheless, several Islamic rituals appear widely practiced.

Public prayer (most commonly in the mosque or at work) is an outwardly visible form of observance. A Western survey of Soviet Germans who emigrated in 1979 reported instances of Central Asian Muslims stopping for prayer at work or wherever they happened to be at prayer times. Dushanbe was one of the places this was observed.[33] Soviet treatment of the subject argues that most Muslims do not pray, whether the required five times a day or fewer times. A study done in Tajikistan (published in 1971) claimed that only 30 percent of believers age forty and older prayed, and that only the elderly prayed a full five times daily.[34] None of this reveals how many people pray privately — in the home or other secluded places; nor does it indicate how often they pray, or their attitudes toward prayer.

Soviet sources downplay the number of Muslims who fast during Ramadan, contending that full compliance is found above all among the rural elderly and that even among them, fewer than half fast the whole month. The survey cited above implies that the largest numbers fast for only a few days at the beginning, middle, and end of the month. One reference to the subject, clearly intended to scare people away from fasting, stated that doctors see many people who

[32] "Maktab va tarbiyai ateisti khonandegon," *Gazetai Muallimon*, January 14, 1984, p. 3; "Maktab va tarbiyai ateisti khonandegon," *Gazetai Muallimon*, January 17, 1984, p. 4; "Maktab va tarbiyai ateisti khonandegon," *Gazetai Muallimon*, January 21, 1984, p. 4; Baimuradov, "Byt' ubezhdennym, umet' ubezhdat'," *Agitator Tadzhikistana*, 1985, no. 15 (August), p. 21; idem, "Sotsializmi mutaraqqi," p. 77; Komilov, "Ba"ze sababhoi," p. 13; A. Safarov, "Tashakkuli jahonbinii ilmi va muboriza ba mukobili khurofoti dini," *Kommunisti Tojikiston*, 1984, no. 4, (April), p. 95.

[33] R. Karklins, "Islam: How Strong is it in the Soviet Union," *Cahiers du Monde Russe et Soviétique*, January-March 1980, pp. 67-68.

[34] Saidbaev, *Islam i obshchestvo*, pp. 201, 287; *Islam v SSSR*, p. 71.

are made seriously ill by the Ramadan cycle of fasting from dawn to dusk and eating a large meal at night. If in fact many are made ill, that points to an even larger number who fast.[35]

Islamic festivals observed in Tajikistan include the Feast of the Sacrifice (*Id-i qurban*) and Muhammad's birthday (*Mawlud*).[36] The pilgrimage to Mecca, the *hajj*, is the one central observance of Islam that has been virtually eliminated in the Soviet Union. One estimate holds that only twenty to twenty-five Central Asians are allowed to make the *hajj* each year. Presumably, these pilgrims are chosen with great care given to their political loyalty.[37]

One of the strongest manifestations of Islam's persistent influence is the performance of life-cycle rituals. These rites, which commonly include the participation of mullahs, are such an integral part of the way of life that they are maintained even by those who are not believing Muslims in a strictly religious sense.[38] Circumcision is reported to be almost universal among Tajiks, Uzbeks, Kirghiz, and Turkmens, among whom it is interpreted as a sign of belonging to the nationality as well as, and in some cases, apart from, its religious significance. Its proponents also defend it on medical grounds. The official Muslim Spiritual Administration of Central Asia and Kazakhstan issued a pronouncement (*fatwa*) against it to no avail.[39]

Traditional weddings are also widespread in Central Asia. Typically, these entail elaborate and lengthy festivities, including customary singing and dancing, the giving of expensive gifts, and the recitation of prayers. The Tajik literary newspaper, *Adabiyot va san"at*, reported in 1985 that it had received many letters indicating that Islamic weddings are the norm in most villages. An officially sponsored Soviet survey conducted in Tajikistan reported that all those questioned believe that a wedding held according to Islam strengthens the marriage. Islamic divorces are also reported in the Soviet Union.[40] Islamic funerals appear to be equally valued, even when the deceased was not a believer. A report indicates that some Muslims could not bring themselves to give up traditional weddings

[35] Saidbaev, *Islam v obshchestvo*, p. 201; *Islam v SSSR*, p. 72; Gh. Odinamamadov, "Farosati tandurusti," *Adabiyot va san"at*, March 28, 1985, p. 12.

[36] M. Yunusov, "Mashvarati muallimoni zabon va adabiyot," *Maktabi Soveti*, 1983, no. 6, (June), p. 55.

[37] D. Shipler, "Moslems in Soviet Caught Between Faith and State," *The New York Times*, January 7, 1979. According to information kindly provided by Professor Edward Lazzerini, the number of Soviet citizens who made the *hajj* between 1971 and 1984 ranged from a low of fourteen in 1984 to a high of twenty-eight in 1979.

[38] Dadabaeva, "Sama soboi," p. 2; "Vazhnaia chast'," pp. 2-3; Saidbaev, *Islam i obshchestvo*, p. 246.

[39] *Islam v SSSR*, pp. 74-75; N. Ashirov, *Musul'manskaia propoved'* (Moscow: Politizdat, 1978), p. 54; A. Khashimov, "Religiia i byt," *Voprosy nauchnogo ateizma*, p. 64.

[40] Dadabaeva, "Konkretno-sotsiologicheskie issledovaniia," pp. 258-59; U. Kuhzod, "Tuiu tamosho," *Adabiyot va san"at*, May 16, 1985, p. 15; S. Fathalloev, "Evoliutsiiai an"anho," *Gazetai Muallimon*, February 28, 1984, p. 4; Gh. Madaliev and I. Ikromov, "Isrofkori ba ki darkor?" *Tojikistoni Soveti*, October 10, 1985, p. 2; Saidbaev, *Islam i obshchestvo*, p. 256.

and funerals even when, on a rational level, they accepted the arguments against such practices.[41]

Soviet Muslims have even devised new rites specific to life in the USSR. Occasions for such rituals include a child's graduation from school or the departure of a young man to do his term of military service. The authorities disapprove of these rites, even though they are connected to the standard transition stages of Soviet life.[42]

Some Islamic practices that persist in the USSR have been outlawed even in some Muslim countries. Wearing the veil has not been permitted since the late 1920s, but many women, especially in villages and in textile factories, wear a large head scarf year round, which authorities consider a symbolic continuation of purdah. The payment of a bride price (*kalym*), often a substantial sum, appears to be widespread in Tajikistan. Arranged marriages occur, as do marriages of underage girls, and even, on rare occasions, polygamy.[43]

Islam continues to encourage what the Soviets call a "feudal" attitude toward women. Girls are still likely to end their schooling far sooner than boys, often without completing middle school. Far fewer women work in industrial, skilled, and white-collar jobs in Tajikistan than in the Soviet Union as a whole. Women are especially under-represented in industrial, skilled, or white collar employment.[44]

Traditional Islamic attitudes toward the family contribute to the high birthrate in Tajikistan and other predominantly Muslim republics, although that is not the sole cause. The population explosion is not unique to Soviet Muslims but is found in many different countries, inhabited by people of various religions, living under diverse political, economic, and social conditions. In Islamic societies, having many children is highly esteemed and of great importance to a woman's status. Muslim families tend to be among the most stable in the Soviet Union. While Tajikistan's marriage rate is close to the all-Union average, the divorce rate is roughly 43 percent of the all-Union rate. Islamic doctrine frowns on abortion, the main form of birth control

[41] Madaliev and Ikromov, "Isrofkori," p. 2; Fathalloev, "Evoliutsiiai an"anho," p. 4; Vagabov, *Islam i voprosy ateisticheskogo vospitaniia* (Moscow: Vysshaia shkola, 1984), p. 108; *Islam v SSSR*, p. 76; "Novye obriady v zhizni trudiashchikhsia," *Agitator Tadzhikistana*, 1978, no. 7 (April), p. 38; Faizibaeva, "Novye obriady — v zhizn'," *Agitator Tadzhikistana*, 1985, no. 3 (February), p. 25.

[42] Jabborova, "Ba"ze problemahoi," p. 88.

[43] Madzhidov, *Osobennosti formirovaniia*, pp. 44-46; "Maktab va tarbiiai ateistii khonandagon," *Gazetai Muallimon*, January 17, 1984, p. 4; *Islam v SSSR*, p. 149; Saidbaev, *Islam i obshchestvo*, p. 255; Radzhabov, "Prichiny sushchestvovaniia perezhitkov proshlogo v soznanii liudei," *Voprosy nauchnogo ateizma*, p. 15.

[44] M. Oqilova, "Fa"oli sotsialii zanoni Tojikiston va omilhoi minba"d vus"at dodani on," *Kommunisti Tojikiston*, 1984, no. 7 (July), pp. 47-48; Shoismatulloev, "Chorsui zindagi," p. 3; Dadabaeva, "Konkretno-sotsiologicheskie," p. 254; Madzhidov, *Osobennosti formirovaniia*, pp. 46-47; "Maktab va tarbiai ateistii khonandagon," January 17, 1984, p. 4, and January 21, 1984, p. 4; M. Zikriyoeva, "Komsomol i ateisti cheskoe vospitanie devushek," *Agitator Tadzhikistana*, 1985, no. 20 (October), p. 19; *Islam v SSSR*, p.135.

for women in the European part of the Soviet Union. Tajikistan has the Soviet Union's highest birthrate — a 3.78 percent annual increase, according to the 1979 census. Other predominantly Muslim republics follow closely behind. Average family size in Tajikistan (5.7 people) is well above that for the Soviet Union as a whole (3.5 people). In parts of rural Tajikistan, families typically have eight to ten children; in some villages sixteen or seventeen children per family is not uncommon.[45]

Official Islam, Soviet-style

Islam survives in part through institutions officially recognized and regulated by the Soviet authorities. Since 1943, there has been a Muslim Spiritual Administration of Central Asia and Kazakhstan, headquartered in Tashkent, the capital of Uzbekistan. (Three similar administrations for other regions of the Soviet Union also exist: for the North Caucasus and Daghestan (northeastern Caucasus), for Transcaucasia, and for European Russia and Siberia. All four regional administrations are under the jurisdiction of a council attached to the All-Union Council of Ministers in Moscow.) The Administration for Central Asia and Kazakhstan has representatives in each of the five republics within its purview. It organizes international Islamic conferences dealing with various themes, including foreign-policy issues of importance to the Soviet Union. One such conference, held in Dushanbe in September 1979, discussed the contribution to the "development of [medieval] Islamic thought on peace and social progress" by Muslims in what is now the USSR and celebrated the start of the fourteenth century of Islam.[46] Participants included thirty-five foreign Muslim clerics representing various countries and Islamic organizations. The conference was intended to convey the messages of opposition to imperialism; praise for arms control, SALT II, the Palestine Liberation Organization, and the revolutions in Iran and Afghanistan; and condemnation of Arabs who favor a separate peace with Israel as traitors to Islam. The conference also praised how well Muslims fared in the Soviet Union.[47]

The Muslim Spiritual Administration of Central Asia and Kazakhstan has published a magazine since 1968, *Muslims of the Soviet East*, initially in Uzbek and Arabic editions, subsequently in Persian, Dari (Kabul Persian), English, and French as well. It publishes reli-

---

[45] Ministerstvo vysshego i srednego spetsial'nogo obrazovaniia SSSR, *Naseleniia SSSR segodnia*, pp. 39-40, Table 2; Tsentral'noe Staticheskoe Upravlenie SSSR, *Chislennost' i sostav naseleniia SSSR* (Moscow: Finansy i statistika, 1984), pp. 220-21; R. Karim, "Imruzi dashti bir"yon," *Sadoi Sharq*, 1982, no. 8, p. 39; Z. Mahmudov, "Tu qadimi, tu javoni," *Tajikistoni Soveti*, December 15, 1982, p. 3; Fedorova, *Goroda Tadzhikistana*, p. 38; Saidbaev, *Islam i obshchestvo*, pp. 257-58.

[46] O. Volgin, "V preddverii XV veka khidzhry," *Novoe Vremia*, 1979, no. 41 (October 5), p. 24.

[47] Ibid.

gious calendars and, on occasion, selections from the Qur'an. According to a 1979 report, six editions of the Qur'an were brought out in the 1960s and 1970s, including a 1976 run of ten thousand. (There are reports of another edition published in the mid-1980s.)[48] This administration also runs the only two *madrasahs* (Islamic seminaries) in the Soviet Union. Mir-i Arab Madrasah, located in Bukhara, Uzbekistan, provides most of the training. As of 1979, its total enrollment was reportedly seventy.[49] Imam Ismail al-Bukhari Madrasah, located in Tashkent, provides more advanced instruction, especially for those who go on to work in the four Spiritual Administrations. Some graduates are allowed to continue their studies abroad in Egypt, Syria, Libya, and Morocco.[50]

An estimated two thousand Muslim mullahs enjoy state authorization and function in officially sanctioned Islamic establishments through the Soviet Union.[51] This is a small number for some 50 million Muslims, and the gap is partially filled by the unofficial clerics (on whom, more below.)

Mosques serve as a center of Muslim community life in many ways — as a place to pray on Fridays or major holy days in symbolic demonstration of membership in the community of believers, as a forum for preachers, as a place for discussion, and as a place to socialize. Some 325 mosques function legally in Central Asia and Kazakhstan; in official parlance, these are categorized as 200 mosques and 125 "small" mosques; Dushanbe has 5 mosques.[52] The officially recognized working mosques in contemporary Central Asia constitute a small fraction of the number that existed before the revolution and are far too few to serve all the practicing Muslims. Soviet sources downplay mosque attendance, implying that it is made up only of retirees and other marginal groups. Nevertheless, attendance at official mosques increases on Fridays and holy days.[53] Muslims compensate for the scarcity of mosques by conducting religious observances in the home (a normal practice in Muslim countries) and by creating their own unofficial mosques.

Through historic preservation, Soviet authorities protect some mosques, *madrasahs*, and saints' tombs. The authorities do not intend that these buildings serve as religious facilities but convert them into tourist attractions, museums, or non-religious teaching centers. While this use would appear to be contrary to the wishes of devout Muslims, the situation is less clear-cut. They appreciate that buildings designed

[48] D. Shipler, "Moslems in Soviet."
[49] Ibid.
[50] A. Bennigsen and C. Lemercier-Quelquejay, "'Official' Islam in the Soviet Union," *Religion in Communist Lands*, Autumn 1979, pp. 153-54.
[51] Ibid., p. 150.
[52] Ibid., p. 151; Shipler, "Moslems in Soviet."
[53] Saidbaev, *Islam i obshchestvo*, p. 238.

for the service of Islam are respected as embodiments of the national heritage. Even officials and non-believers value the buildings in that sense. [54]

Only a small proportion of Tajikistan's historic sites have been preserved, and the quality of the work done is too often inexpert. Even if flawed, preservation is better than what most sites in the republic have endured — decay, demolition, or conversion to profane use (such as storage warehouses or offices). Islamic sites preserved in Tajikistan in recent years include mosques, saints' tombs, and *madrasahs* dating from the tenth to the twentieth centuries.[55] The continued existence of these buildings is in itself a symbol of the Islamic heritage. That many of them are open to visitors makes it possible for Muslims to pay their respects, even if overt prayer is forbidden. One Soviet source indicates that pilgrimages to tombs and other revered places continue even after these have been reclassified as architectural monuments.[56]

The leaders of official Islam try to demonstrate that their religion is a harmonious component of Soviet life. In part, they do this by giving fulsome support to Soviet foreign policy in general and with regard to issues involving the Islamic world, such as the Arab-Israeli dispute or the Soviet invasion of Afghanistan. They also adapt their interpretation of Islam to fit the constraints of life in the Soviet Union. Often called "modernizing" Islam, this effort is associated closely with the Muslim Spiritual Administration for Central Asia and Kazakhstan. Much more than a corruption of Islam to please the authorities in Moscow, it is a strategy of modifying nonessential elements of Islamic practice to buy leeway for Islam to continue to function as a religious system.

Modernization of Islam is not simply an adaptation to the requirements of communism. There have been many modernizers in various parts of the Islamic world, including the Russian Empire, since the nineteenth century. (Nor are such concerns unique to Islam.) As propounded today in the Soviet Union, modernism emphasizes the relaxation of ritual obligations and the reconciliation of Islam with communist doctrine. As such, modernized Islam offers no challenge to the political order. It does not object to Muslims joining the Communist party so long as they remain Muslims at heart.[57] Full compliance with the five pillars of Islam (the profession of faith, prayer

[54] Ibid., pp. 229, 238; R. Muqimov, "Merosi ajdodi mo," *Adabiyot va san"at*, January 17, 1985, p. 13; O. Musoev, "Oina ta"rikh," *Sadoi Sharq*, 1985, no. 9, pp. 42-43.

[55] "Hifzi yodgoriho — vazifai hama," *Tojikistoni Soveti*, May 27, 1986, p. 1; A. Toatov, "Zaboni guyoni ta"rikh," *Tojikistoni Soveti*, February 16, 1986, p. 2; Muqimov, "Merosi ajdodi mo," p. 13; O. Musoev, "Oinai ta"rikh," p. 42; M. Mamadnazarov, "Paivandi asrho," *Adabiyot va san"at*, June 27, 1985, p. 10; TadzhikTA, "Sokhranit' kul'turnoe nasledie," *Kommunist Tadzhikistana*, June 3, 1986, p. 2.

[56] Saidbaev, *Islam i obshchestvo*, p. 234.

[57] Bennigsen and Lemercier-Quelquejay, "'Official' Islam," p. 156.

five times daily, alms-giving, the Ramadan fast, and the pilgrimage to Mecca) is not required. To remain a Muslim, it is sufficient not to repudiate the faith.[58] The Central Asian Islamic establishment argues that the social values of the religion coincide with — indeed, anticipated — those of communism with regard to social justice, equality, brotherhood, and peace. Therefore, to be a practicing Muslim in the contemporary Soviet Union is to work for goals that are beneficial to Soviet society.[59]

Moscow reacts with ambivalence. Given that many citizens continue to identify with Islam, the leadership prefers an interpretation of the religion's teachings that accepts socialism and harmonizes with it. The Soviets probably see this form of Islam playing a positive role by encouraging citizens who are believers to support the regime. Moreover, when discussing conditions in countries of "socialist orientation" where Islam is strong, Soviet experts contend that an interpretation that stresses the similarities between Islam and socialism is a valuable tool for mobilizing the masses in support of a socialist transformation.[60] As one prominent Soviet Orientalist noted, "Sincere advocates of scientific socialism sometimes turn to Islam to put the substance of socialist teaching into the language of the politically undeveloped masses in the name of the toilers' social liberation."[61]

The Soviets cannot openly admit that the same logic applies in the Soviet Union, a fully socialist state, yet it is possible that this argument does influence the leadership's attitude toward domestic Islam. The favorable discussion of this approach in recent Soviet publications aimed at mass domestic audiences hints that this might be the case.[62]

At the same time, the regime regards any system of values other than Marxism-Leninism as competition. If the treatment of Islamic modernism in Soviet sources is any indication, the adaptive strategy

[58] Ashirov, "Musul'manskaia propoved'," p. 32; A. Safarov, "Tashakkuli jahonbinii," p. 93.

[59] Ashirov, "Musul'manskaia propoved'," pp. 20, 25, 31-32; A. Akhmedov, *Sotsial'naia doktrina islama* (Moscow: Politizdat, 1982), p. 131; Madzhidov, "Modernistskie tendentsii v islame v usloviiakh sotsializma," *Voprosy nauchnogo ateizma* pp. 226, 229-32; M. Sokhibnazarov, "Ateisticheskomu vospitaniiu — nastupatel'nost'," *Agitator Tadzhikistana*, 1981, no. 15 (August), p. 18.

[60] M. Atkin, "Soviet Attitudes Toward Shi'ism and Social Protest," in J. R. I. Cole and N.R. Keddie,eds., *Shi'ism and Social Protest* (New Haven: Yale University Press, 1986), pp. 282, 284; L. R. Polonskaia, "Sovremennye musul'manskie ideinye techeniia," Akademiia Nauk SSSR, Institut Vostokovedenie, *Islam: problemy ideologii, prava, politiki i ekonomiki* (Moscow: Nauka. Glavnaia redaktsiia Vostochnoi literatury, 1985), pp. 22-23; A. Vasil'ev, "Islam i politicheskaia bor'ba," *Pravda*, April 14, 1980, p. 6.

[61] Z. I. Levin, "O predelakh radikal'nosti 'islamskogo sotsializma' (arabskie strany)," *Islam: problemy ideologii, prava, politiki i ekonomiki*, p. 97.

[62] Akhmedov, *Sotsial'naia doktrina islama*, pp. 26, 58-60, 102-103 (the book was pubished in a run of 100,000 copies); S. Aliev, "Islam i sovremennost'," *Agitator Tadzhikistana*, 1982, no. 21 (November) pp. 21-22; E. Iurkov, "Pod pritselom SShA," *Agitator Tadzhikistana*, 1984, no. 3 (February), pp. 31-32; Vasil'ev, "Islam i politicheskaia bor'ba," p. 6; "Kto podnimaet zelonoe znamia," *Komsomolskaia Pravda*, June 30, 1982, p. 2; G. Kerimov, "Islam i politika," *Molodoi Kommunist*, 1982, no. 12 (1982), pp. 96-97.

has actually helped Islam hold on to its following, especially among the educated and the young. To check the influence of modernist Islam, Soviet propagandists and scholars insist that this interpretation disguises the true gulf between the values of Islam and communism; in fact, Islam traditionally championed intolerance, social inequality, and aggression.[63] In all likelihood, this criticism does not reflect grave concern that modernist Islam constitutes a threat to Soviet authority. Modernist Islam has to be the target of criticism, regardless of particulars, for the party cannot accept, on principle, any ideology other than Marxism-Leninism.

In the end, for all the official mullahs' accommodation of the Soviet regime, ordinary Muslims in Central Asia probably see them as serving the interests of Islam.[64] But there is more to Islam in Central Asia than official Islam. A deeply rooted folk Islam, loosely structured and standing outside the system of controls, exists, too.

Unofficial Islam

Varieties of Belief. Those aspects of Islam not regulated by the Soviet state have been the focus of increased interest in the West since the 1970s. According to Soviet usage, "unofficial Islam" refers not to a cohesive underground but rather to any and all religious manifestations not supervised by one of the four Muslim Spiritual Administrations. Above all, "unofficial Islam" encompasses varieties of popular religion that have evolved among ordinary believers, which often include elements of earlier religions that survived by becoming in some fashion Islamic. The most active unofficial clerics who have been publicly identified in recent years have all been advocates of unwavering devotion to Islam; many are Sufis (mystics) but some identify themselves as Wahhabis (followers of the puritanical anti-Sufi doctrine found in its original form in Saudi Arabia). These Wahhabis call for a return to the simplicity and piety of early Islam and decry what they consider later corruptions, including Sufism.[65] Some Western observers argue that Sufism is the locus of "rampant anti-Russian nationalism" with "a fundamentalist colouring" and that it is well regarded by Soviet Muslims, even those who are not Sufis

---

[63] Komilov, "Omili muhimi tashakkuli e"tiqodi ateisti," *Maktabi Soveti*, 1983, no. 5 (May), p. 24; Jabborova, "Ba"ze problemahoi," p. 89; Boimurodov, "Sotsializmi mutaraqqi," p. 75; M. Khalmukhamedov, "O chem govoriat," p. 59; Ashirov, "Musul'manskaia propoved'," pp. 31-33; Sokhibnazarov, "Ateisticheskomy vospitaniiu," p. 18; Madzhidov, "Modernistskie tendentsii," pp. 228, 231-33.

[64] J. Critchlow, "Islam and Nationalism in Soviet Central Asia," *Religion and Nationalism in Soviet and East European Politics* (Durham, N. C.: Duke University Press, 1984), p. 111.

[65] Sanginov, "Ashki nadomat," p. 4; V. Rabiev, "V klass . . . s koranom?" *Kommunist Tadzhikistana*, January 31, 1987, p.2.

themselves. [66] Be that as it may, there is much more to unofficial Islam in Central Asia than its political coloration.

Sufism is remarkable for its variety. What began as an individual quest for spiritual enlightenment became organized movements between the eleventh and fifteenth centuries. Major orders evolved, each with its own practices for achieving mystic exaltation. Sufis played a major role in winning converts to Islam in Central Asia and the North Caucasus, in good part because of their willingness to absorb and adapt aspects of the converts' previous beliefs. Sufism holds no monopoly on ways to seek the aid of supernatural powers. Although many springs, trees, and other features of the Central Asian landscape associated with saints latterly became linked to Sufism, other features are still venerated as purely natural phenomena, much as they had been in pre-Islamic times.[67] Some unofficial clerics in contemporary Central Asia are actually shamans who perpetuate ancient pagan practices under the thinnest veneer of Islam.[68] As two Western anthropologists who have worked in Afghanistan and elsewhere in the Islamic world report:

Perhaps Western Orientalists have considered Sufism in its myriad forms to be the exhaustive popular response to the formalities of orthodox Islam. Yet as anyone knows who has been attentive to the patterns of behavior and belief in Middle Eastern villages (or towns, or cities), these worlds are full of holy men and women, shrines, incarnate forces of good and evil, evil eyes, incantations, and ceremonies, all of which help to make up a cosmological outlook in which formal Islam plays an important but by no means exclusive role.[69]

Varieties of Practice. Sufism is really many different things in terms of its ideas, practices, and structure. It has ranged "from the primitive nature-mysticism, spirit-raising, and power-cults of folk religion to the refined, desiccated reaches of philosophical monism."[70] It may be quietist or combative, and sometimes a single order has been both at different times and in different places.[71] A single Sufi order could also vary considerably from one area to another in terms of its tenets and rituals.[72] For most of its existence, Sufism has been characterized by syncretism, drawing on ideas and practices from

[66] Bennigsen and S. E. Wimbush, *Mystics and Commissars* (Berkeley and Los Angeles: University of California Press, 1985), pp. 104, 106, 109.

[67] O. Alaev, "Pochemu pokloniaiutsia mazaram?" *Nauka i religiia*, 1979, no. 7, p. 20.

[68] Bennigsen and Lemercier-Quelquejay, *L'Islam en Union Soviétique*, p. 185.

[69] R. A. Fernea and E. W. Fernea, "Variation in Religious Observance among Islamic Women," in N. R. Keddie, ed., *Scholars, Saints, and Sufis* (Berkeley and Los Angeles: University of California Press, 1972), p. 391.

[70] J. S. Trimingham, *The Sufi Orders in Islam* (Oxford: The Clarendon Press, 1971), p. 230. For a similar assessment, see E. Gellner, *Muslim Society* (Cambridge: Cambridge University Press, 1981), pp. 49-50.

[71] Trimingham, *The Sufi Orders*, p. 240; M. N. Shahrani, "Causes and Context of Responses to the Saur Revolution in Badakhshan," in M. N. Shahrani and R. L. Canfield, eds., *Revolutions and Rebellions in Afghanistan* (Berkeley: University of California, Institute of International Studies, 1984), p. 151.

[72] Trimingham, *The Sufi Orders*, p. 220.

dissident strains of Islam and from outside Islam. One order, the Vaisiyya, an offshoot of the Naqshbandiyya, preached a combination of Wahhabi puritanism, Tatar nationalism, and socialism, first of the populist, later of the Bolshevik variety. The order's second leader died fighting on the Bolshevik side in the Civil War.[73]

The term "order" (*tariqa*) implies the kind of tight organization that rarely exists in practice in Sufism. Sufi rhetoric encourages this misperception. The standard description of the authority of a Sufi master over his disciples emphasizes the total submission of the latter to the former. However, that is only the ideal; in practice there is usually much less control.[74] Some Sufi orders are decentralized, including the Naqshbandiyya, traditionally one of the most important in Central Asia. The same is true of Sufism among Sunni Muslims in an adjoining region of Afghanistan.[75] Traditionally, Sufism included itinerant dervishes who had no close ties to any order. There is no evidence, at least for Tajikistan, to indicate whether some of the itinerant Sufis reported to be there now belong to this category.

Some scholars see Sufism in Central Asia as closely linked to tribal and clan structures, and most closely where those structures have survived more nearly intact, especially among the Turkmens and the Kazakhs.[76] This is entirely plausible, given that this linkage existed in Central Asia before 1917 and was a common phenomenon in the Islamic world in general.[77] If this is the situation in Central Asia, it poses a grave obstacle to the Sufi orders' potential to spearhead anti-Soviet or anti-Russian sentiments beyond the narrow limits of their own particular clan or tribal following.

In broad terms, adherence to Sufism entails two different levels of commitment. While a small number of adherents pursue their particular variety of Sufism as their primary activity, the vast majority learn some Sufi teachings and ritual forms, but not as much as the full-time adepts; they follow the Sufi practices only to the extent that these can be integrated into everyday life.[78]

Some observers see Sufism in contemporary Central Asia as strong in the countryside and contrast it politically as well as geographically with the largely urban "official" Islam.[79] But the contrast should not be overstated. In much of the Muslim world, Sufism has

---

[73] Bennigsen and Lemercier-Quelquejay, *L'Islam en Union Soviétique*, pp. 63, 90.

[74] Gellner, *Muslim Society*, p. 50.

[75] Bennigsen, "Soviet Muslims and the World of Islam," *Problems of Communism*, March-April 1980, p. 39; Bennigsen and Wimbush, *Mystics and Commissars*, p. 75; Canfield, "Islamic Coalitions in Bamyan: A Problem in Translating Afghan Political Culture," *Revolutions and Rebellions in Afghanistan*, pp. 219, 221-24.

[76] Bennigsen, "Soviet Islam," p. 66; Bennigsen and Lemercier-Quelquejay, "L'Islam parallèle en Union Soviétique," *Cahiers du Monde Russie et Soviétique*, January-March, 1980, p. 56.

[77] Saidbaev, *Islam i obshchestvo*, p. 79; Triminghan, *The Sufi Orders*, p. 234.

[78] Trimingham, *The Sufi Orders*, pp. 27, 175-76.

[79] Bennigsen and Lemercier-Quelquejay, "'Official' Islam," pp. 152-53.

traditionally been a rural and tribal alternative to the established, legalistic Islam of the cities, in large part because the Sufis' outreach to the villagers and nomadic tribesmen was greater than that of urban, establishment Islam. Tribe members commonly did not see themselves practicing a divergent form of the religion, believing their Islam akin to urban, establishment Islam (even when this was not the case).[80]

An account of Sufi activity in Tajikistan from the early 1960s depicts Sufis and mullahs cooperating to build an unauthorized mosque and compelling the local inhabitants to observe Sufi and standard Islamic practices, including prayer, the Ramadan fast, and the Sufi *dhikr* (practices in pursuit of mystical enlightenment).[81] Moreover, Sufis traditionally ministered to many ordinary Muslims, urban and rural, guiding them spiritually, providing leadership, and helping their poor and ill.[82] These functions are still carried out among the Tajiks and Uzbeks of contemporary Afghanistan.[83]

For our purposes, the most important dimension of Sufism is not the sophisticated mysticism practiced by the Sufi adepts but the Sufi embodiment of folk Islam. Indeed, Saidbaev considers this an especially tenacious aspect of Islam.[84] Some Western experts regard Sufism's folk Islam as backsliding toward pre-Islamic beliefs, "archaic forms of primitive cults close to ancient shamanism," brought about by the scarcity of mullahs representing establishment Islam.[85] And while it is true that Sufism as now practiced in Central Asia incorporates elements of the region's pre-Islamic religions, dismissing this as regressive misses the point. The ability to assimilate elements of other beliefs has been one of Sufism's most prominent and powerful traits for a millenium. It has enabled Sufis to play a crucial role converting peoples in the borderlands of the Muslim world and has made folk Islam central to the living faith of millions of ordinary Muslims. By all indications, it retains that importance today for Muslims in rural parts of Central Asia.

There are enough unofficial Islamic mullahs functioning in Tajikistan for the Communist party first secretary of Tajikistan, Q. M. Mahkamov, to consider the matter worth discussing at his party's Twentieth Congress in January 1986 and the plenum of its Central Committee in April of the same year.[86] He told the Congress that some unofficial clerics apparently perform routine clerical activities

---

[80] Gellner, *Muslim Society*, pp. 115, 130.
[81] Safarov, *Boqimondahoi parastishi eshonho va rohhoi bartaraf kardani onho dar Tojikiston* (Dushanbe: Akademiia Nauk Tadzhikistana, 1965), p. 7.
[82] Trimingham, *The Sufi Orders*, pp. 215, 219, 229, 230-31, 234, 237.
[83] Shahrani, "Responses to the Saur Revolution," pp. 150-51.
[84] Saidbaev, *Islam i obshchestvo*, p. 38.
[85] Bennigsen and Lemercier-Quelquejay, *L'Islam en Union Soviétique*, p. 185
[86] *Kommunist Tadzhikistana*, January 26, 1986, p. 3; TadzhikTA, "Pretvorim v zhizn'," p. 3.

like their officially registered counterparts, leading prayers in unofficial mosques, giving instruction in Islamic doctrine, and encouraging believers to observe standard Islamic practices.[87] Some, however, are clearly practitioners of folk Islam.

A Tajik publication from the early 1960s provides unusually explicit detail about Sufi activities in the republic. Though unverifiable and openly hostile in intent, one can ignore the defamatory rhetoric about Sufis swindling and misleading people, and concentrate instead on the many descriptions of Sufi practices and functions, which correspond closely to the traditional range of activities. One man discussed is a Sufi master, or *ishan*, named Azizkhontura Abdunabiev, who lived on a *sovkhoz* in southwestern Tajikistan from 1948 until at least 1961. Abdunabiev built a mosque near his house and led prayers there. He also built a traditional Sufi convent in the Central Asian style (a *khonaqoh*) near his house.[88] During Ramadan each year he hosted the fast-breaking meal in his house to which believers were invited. They stayed until dawn and then performed the *dhikr*. Abdunabiev attracted a following of many adepts, or *murids*, whom he assigned as his representatives; they in turn recruited more *murids*. Two or three times a year he visited the *raions* where these representatives lived. On a trip to five or so *raions* in 1960, he traveled with an entourage of some ten persons, collected alms, and conducted the *dhikr*. Abdunabiev also received the pious in need, such as the sick, childless women, and various unfortunates, and received gifts from them in return for his prayers. According to the author of this account, there are many other *ishans* like Abdunabiev.[89]

As this story indicates, Sufi adepts recruit some of the unofficial clergy. These may be informal, part-time mullahs who are no more than pious men versed enough in the ceremonies to lead them as the occasion warrants and offer instruction in Islam. Some may be men who became mullahs on retirement; others may still be employed in conventional secular jobs. Saidbaev thinks many mullahs, possessing considerable ability and attractive personalities, can readily influence others.[90] If the hostile accounts in the Tajikistan press are at all accurate, unofficial mullahs sometimes occupy positions of considerable influence in villages. In addition, some lead prayers in the many unofficial mosques, even in Dushanbe.[91]

---

[87] TadzhikTA, "Pretvorim v zhizn'," p. 3; T. Khurshedova, "Vospityvat' primerami iz zhizni" *Agitator Tadzhikistana*, 1985, no. 23 (December), pp. 25-26.

[88] A *khonaqoh* could be an imposing structure several stories tall, with a large, domed central chamber surrounded by small rooms, or a humble structure little different from an ordinary house but having one room which contains some religious artifacts and could accommodate the assembled sufis.

[89] A. Safarov, *Boqimondahoi*, pp. 6-7.

[90] Khalmukhamedov, "O chem govoriat," p. 57; N. Safarov, "Tarbiyai ateisti," p. 2; Saidbaev, *Islam i obshchestvo*, pp. 214-15.

[91] TadzhikTA, "Pretvorim v zhizn'," p. 3; Boimurodov, "Sotsializmi mutaraqqi," p. 77; "Maktab va tarbiyai ateistii khonandagon," *Gazetai Muallimon*, January 14, 1984, p. 3.

Unofficial mosques exist in sufficient numbers to displease authorities in Tajikistan. A recent Tajik-language play about Islam, *Dar Chorsu* (At the crossroads), depicts a village in which the unofficial mullah and his followers turn the local tea house into their mosque. This happens in real life, with tea houses, village clubs, and other facilities. On one *sovkhoz* not far from the provincial capital of Qurghonteppa (Kurgan-Tiube), the residents contributed money and labor to build twenty-two mosques masquerading as tea houses.[92]

Unofficial holy places, *mazars*, survive and are still popular pilgrimage sites. Some are buildings, such as saints' tombs or reliquaries; others are natural phenomena (springs, trees, or an unusual natural feature). On visiting holy places, the pious pray, make sacrifices, and tie strips of cloth to tree branches. The designation of new holy sites in rural Tajikistan reflects the continued popularity of this institution, which Tajikistani authorities found so widespread that they published a pamphlet for use in schools to debunk *mazars*. Soviet authorities have tried to stop the pilgrimages by converting some of the sites to secular usage, such as resorts and sanatoriums. But Muslims find ways to make the pilgrimages, sometimes in the guise of taking a group vacation.[93]

One holy place, Khoja Bolo, in Hisor (Gissar) *raion*, west of Dushanbe, seems typical of many of its kind. The site has two springs and a holy grave of some sort that is credited with curative powers. Khoja Bolo is popular among young people and families, who come from surrounding villages and Uzbekistan. The faithful believe that seeing a fish living in one of the springs three times cures numerous ailments. A mullah on the scene, dressed in the traditional turban and robe, will pray for someone's cure. An old woman also presides but has no contact with the mullah. She sits between two plane trees that reportedly mark the holy grave and, surrounded by female believers, also prays for the ill.[94]

The popularity of these pilgrimage sites may be connected to the ban on pilgrimages to Mecca; in effect, the local sites substitute for this unattainable destination.[95] That these pilgrimages fit the continuing tradition of folk Islam is also a powerful factor, for they

[92] O. Vose","Dar Chorsu'-i andeshaho," p. 3; TadzhikTA, "Pretvorim v zhizn'," p. 3; Surkov, "Komandirovka v rai," p. 4; A. Safarov, *Boqimondahoi*, p. 35. Sanginov, "Ashki nadomat," p.4.

[93] "Ifshoi sirri mazorho," *Maktabi Soveti*, 1985, no. 9 (May), pp. 62-63; O. Alaev, "Pochemu pokloniaiutsia mazaram?" p. 21. A. Mukhtorov, "'Mui muborak' chist?" *Tojikistoni Soveti*, December 27, 1985, p. 4; "Maktab va tarbiyai ateistii khonandagon," *Gazetai Muallimon*, January 17, 1984, p. 4; A. Mirbabaev, "'Tainy' rodnikov," *Agitator Tadzhikistana*, 1984, no. 13, (July), pp. 27-29. Saidbaev, *Islam i obshchestvo*, p. 234; M. Dzhurakulov, "Ateizmu — nastupatel'nost'," *Agitator Tadzhikistana*, 1982, no. 19 (October), p. 26.

[94] L. Kolbina, "Sviatoe mesto," *Komsomolets Tadzhikistana*, August 5, 1983; Mirbabaev, "'Tainy' rodnikov," pp. 27-29; Madzhidov, "Vospityvat' ubezhdennykh ateistov," *Agitator Tadzhikistana*, 1984, no. 5 (March), p. 27.

[95] Bennigsen and Lemercier-Quelquejay, *L'Islam en Union Soviétique*, p. 185.

combine pre-Islamic nature worship with the cult of saints, which Sufism assimilated in the Middle Ages.

Various forms of folk Islam remain extremely important to ordinary believers as a response to the hazards of everyday life. In rural Tajikistan and other Central Asian republics, people still commonly turn to local mullahs, *ishans*, and other folk healers to cure diseases and infertility, ensure the birth of a son, save accident victims, safeguard loved ones, offer protection from natural disasters, and fulfill miscellaneous wishes.[96]

Women are an important part of folk Islam's constituency. For example, more than 70 percent of the pilgrims to *mazars* in Tajikistan are women, according to an estimate by the Soviet authorities.[97] The extensive involvement of women in folk Islam has important political implications. The woman's traditional role in Islam is caring for the family. When family members are in peril, the woman seeks a remedy through folk Islam. If a couple has no children, the woman is presumed to be responsible and looks to folk Islam for a cure.

Folk Islam allows women far more scope for involvement than does establishment Islam, which excluded women from mosques in pre-revolutionary Central Asia. The old woman at the Khoja Bolo *mazar* who says prayers for the ill and has her own following offers a glimpse into the parallel world of women's Islam, in which holy women have as much of a role as holy men. Although Muslim women in Tajikistan say the standard Islamic prayers, some of them still follow special rites of their own, honoring not only Fatima, the Prophet's daughter, but also women like Bibi Mushkilkusho (Lady problem-solver). Some of these observances are performed at *mazars* and others in the home, sometimes by large gatherings of women while the men of the household are away.[98]

One might question whether the Soviet sources on which foreigners must rely for information deliberately exaggerate the role of women in folk Islam in order to divert attention from its opposition politics. Given that Western studies of several Muslim countries describe a similar situation, it seems likely that the Soviet sources are accurate in reporting on Central Asia at least in this regard.[99]

---

[96] N. Baimuradov, "Byt' ubezhdennym," p. 21; Boimurodov, "Sotsializmi mutaraqqi," p. 77; Odinamamadov, "Farosati tandurusti," p. 12; A. Safarov, *Boqimonadhoi*, pp. 6, 8-10, 13-14; O.A. Sukhareva, "Perezhitki demonologii i shamanstva u ravninnykh Tadzhikov," *Domusul'manskie verovaniia i obriady v Srednei Azii* (Moscow: Nauka, Glavnaia redakstiia Vostochnoi literatury, 1975), p. 10; Madzhidov, *Osobennosti formirovaniia*, pp. 43-44, 54-55; G. Mavlonov, "Tashakuli e"tikodi ilmi," *Gazetai Muallimon*, May 4, 1985, p. 2; G. Snesarev, "Shamany i 'sviatye' v Srednei Azii," *Nauka i religiia*, no. 12 (1976), pp. 31-33; Saidbaev, *Islam i obshchestvo*, pp. 212-13; and Vagabov, *Islam i voprosy*, p. 112.

[97] Madzhidov, *Osobennosti formirovaniia*, p. 43; Dadabaeva, "Konkretno-sotsiologicheskie issledovaniia," p. 256.

[98] Madzhidov, *Osobennosti formirovaniia*, p. 48; Snesarev, "Shamany i 'sviatye'," pp. 32, 34.

[99] D. H. Dwyer, "Women, Sufism, and Decision-Making," in L. Beck and N. Keddie,

The extensive involvement of women in folk Islam has important implications for the political significance of Sufism. Historically, Muslim women had little role to play in politics. By all indications, women's participation in folk Islamic practices in Tajikistan is still motivated by the same non-political concerns that drew them in the past. Thus, the strength of folk Islam in Tajikistan, based as it is to such an extent on women's involvement, is not a reliable gauge of Sufism's potential as a political underground.

Although Sufism and other forms of folk Islam are a vital force in the lives of many Muslims in Tajikistan, it is difficult to assess their political strength. Obviously, whatever political dissent might exist would have to be secretive, and therefore hard to detect, given the constraints of the Soviet system. This said, there is reason to doubt that Sufism plays, or can play, a powerful political role in Tajikistan or elsewhere in the USSR. Sufism means too many different things to different adherents, and too much of it has nothing to do with politics. Sufis also lack an organized, integrated structure. For example, in the southern half of Central Asia, Turkmens have a long history of hostility towards Uzbeks and Tajiks, a mutual involvement in Sufism not withstanding.

Faith and Politics. While Soviet authorities disapprove of Sufism, as they must disapprove of any focus of loyalty that competes with the Communist party and the Soviet state, their statements on this subject do not sound unduly alarmist. The regime seems no more worried about this than about a host of other challenges. Perhaps they have underestimated the danger, though Soviet authorities normally overestimate such perils. Certainly the authorities criticize Sufism, but they also treat Sufis favorably — usually in conjunction with the past, hardly ever the present — when this suits their purposes. But discussions of the past are important; the Soviet educational and propaganda systems routinely use it to make points about the present. When M. V. Vagabov, a veteran atheist propagandist in the Caucasus and at Moscow State University, writes in a book used in courses on atheism that Shamil led an "anti-colonial war" in the Caucasus, he may be playing with fire, but in Soviet parlance he is complimenting this charismatic Sufi leader who led the fight against Russia's conquest of the Caucasus.[100]

There are other indications, too. In recent years, Soviet scholars and Tajikistani publications aimed at the intelligentsia and the broader public have repeatedly portrayed Sufism in association with anti-feudal movements, free-thinking criticism of Islam, and human-

---

eds., *Women in the Muslim World* (Cambridge, Mass.: Harvard University Press, 1978), pp. 587-91, 593, 594, 596-97; Fernea and Fernea, "Observance among Islamic Women," pp. 389, 396, 399; and Trimingham, *The Sufi Orders*, p. 232.

[100] Vagabov, *Islam i voprosy*, p. 31.

ism. For example, Bobojon Ghafurov, long the arbiter of Tajik culture, portrayed medieval Sufism in Central Asia as composed of two contrasting movements, one supporting the status quo, the other advocating the interests of urban artisans opposed to the existing order. The Sufi movement that represented the latter advocated equality of property and at times came close to realizing that objective. Ghafurov considered this kind of Sufism a progressive force in its time. He also praised Sufi literature for its emphasis on human worth.[101]

Soviet publications describe Sufism, even in modern times, as a form of mass Islam, and contrast it favorably to establishment Islam, depicted as hierarchical and elitist. Thus, Marietta Stepaniants, a leading Soviet scholar of Islamic thought, depicts contemporary Sufism as a means — on some occasions — to express social and political protest, criticism of establishment Islam, and resistance to Westernization. Of course, Sufism is also criticized for cooperating with the "feudal" elite and disparaged for losing many of its good qualities as it evolved over time.[102] But, while criticism is to be expected in Soviet treatments of this subject, most noteworthy are the numerous positive comments.[103]

The Islam that survives in Tajikistan has preserved much of its traditional nature while certain aspects, usually the more formal, have been adapted to the constraints of the Soviet system. There is good reason to believe that Islam retains a significant following among a broad spectrum of the population, although there is no way to ascertain the size of the believing Muslim community. Many Muslims observe Islam as of old, and not in the spirit of the new, militant fundamentalism. Even those aspects of Islam that are the least regulated and enjoy strong popular support have too apolitical a character and too diffuse a structure to rally believers under an anti-Soviet political banner.

---

[101] Ghafurov, *Tojikon*, vol. 1, pp. 593-95.

[102] M. T. Stepaniants, "Istoricheskie sud'by sufizma," *Voprosy filosofii*, no. 6 (1980), pp. 101, 109-10, 111.

[103] For other assessments of the positive and negative sides of Sufism, see Q. Vosiev, "Oini javonmardi," *Sadoi Sharq*, 1984, no. 4, pp. 116, 118, 119, 121-22; N. Rahmatulloev, "Shahdi khiradi mashriq," *Sadoi Sharq*, 1984, no. 5, p. 134; M. Shahidi, "Tazzodhoi Pokiston," *Sadoi Sharq*, 1985, no. 6, p. 48; Siddiqov, "Zaboni guyo," p. 14; A. Tursunov, "Mukolamai notamom," *Gazetai Muallimon*, November 20, 1984, p. 4; A.I. Ionova, "Izuchenie Sovetskimi uchenymi islama," *Religii mira 1984*, p. 263; Iu. D. Dzhumbaev, "K izucheniiu istorii eticheskoi mysli narodov Srednei Azii," *Voprosy filosofii*, 1984, no. 11, p. 128.

Islam's Persistence
in the Soviet Union

Before one can gauge the likely impact of Islamic activism in Iran and Afghanistan on Muslims in Soviet Central Asia, it is first necessary to understand the internal as well as external causes of Islam's strength, persistence, and adaptability during seven decades of Soviet rule. The Soviet authorities have long wrestled with this question. Official Soviet statements cite domestic as well as external factors: the strength of entrenched traditions; the historic backwardness of the Muslim regions in the USSR; lower levels of employment outside the home; and the routine charge of imperialist propaganda.[1]

Domestic Causes

The Quest for Spiritual Values. One of the causes of Islam's survival is not unique to Muslims but rather reflects the quest of many Soviet citizens for a more meaningful system of values than that offered by Moscow's version of Marxism-Leninism. Some Russians, especially members of the intelligentsia, view Orthodoxy as a repository of the Russian heritage and an ethical guide, and dismiss atheism for making no contribution in either area.[2] In the Muslim regions, where religion seems to retain a stronger influence than elsewhere, it is even more common to look to faith for ethical and spiritual guidance. This augments or replaces the official ideology of the regime, as the case may be.

The Persistence of the Traditional Social Environment. Life in Central Asia favors the survival of traditional attitudes because it favors the persistence of the traditional way of life. A majority of the indigenous peoples live in rural areas and engage in agriculture and animal husbandry. Villages tend to be composed overwhelmingly of a single nationality (for example, rural Tajiks and Uzbeks are likely to live apart). Few Russians live in the countryside and those who

---

[1] Vagabov, *Islam i voprosy*, pp. 105, 109, 112-16; Saidbaev, *Islam i obshchestvo*, 210-11, 251.

[2] G. Hosking, "The Politics of Literature," in J. Cracraft, ed., *The Soviet Union Today* (Chicago: Bulletin of the Atomic Scientists, 1983), p. 274; P. A. Lucey, "Religion," in ibid., p. 297.

do tend to live in their own villages. Tajikistan has some three thousand villages which lie dispersed among several unconnected valleys. The regime's propaganda efforts in the countryside remain weak. Villagers tend not to move to the cities and those who do retain strong links with their home villages. According to the 1979 census, 80.7 percent of Tajikistan's rural inhabitants are still living in their place of birth.[3]

Urbanization and industrialization have not changed conditions as much as Soviet authorities might wish. A significant proportion of the industrial working class in Central Asia is employed in traditional handicraft trades (such as the textile and garment industries) and in low-skilled construction trades. Members of the indigenous nationalities are, to be sure, employed in Tajikistan's more modern industries, but many in that labor force are Slavs and others who come from outside the republic. Most Central Asians categorized as workers came from the countryside and retain strong ties to the village way of life, including religion. They usually live in mono-ethnic quarters of cities inhabited predominantly by people who came originally from the same rural area. In some republics (but not Tajikistan) where clan affiliation has survived, that too is mirrored in urban settlement patterns. Many of Tajikistan's cities still have the characteristics of pre-industrial cities, where administration, commerce, handicrafts, and the sale and processing of agricultural products prevail.[4] Like other Central Asian nationalities, Tajiks are highly endogamous. On the rare occasions when they marry non-Tajiks, the spouse is most likely to be an Uzbek.[5]

When young Tajikistani villagers do move to the cities, they are as likely to influence people there in favor of religion as they themselves are to be influenced by atheism.[6] Under these conditions it is not surp rising that public opinion requires at least outward conformity with Islamic practices and social sensibiliies. Those who observe the principal rites of Islam are well regarded in their community; conversely, popular opinion still considers atheism to be

[3] Jabborova, "Ba"ze problemahoi," p. 89; "San"ati yagonai sermillat," *Madaniyati Tojikiston*, October 21, 1983, p. 2; Sh. Ismailov and M. Kleandrov, "Roli takomuloti qonunguzori dar ijroi programmai ozuqavori," *Kommunisti Tojikiston*, December 1983, p. 26; O. Ahmadov, "Talaboti khojagii khalqi RSS Tojikiston ba quvvai kori va problemahoi ta"minoti on," *Kommunisti Tojikiston*, August 1985, p. 70; *Islam v SSSR*, p. 116; Saidbaev, *Islam i obshchestvo*, pp. 222, 225; Tsentral'noe Staticheskoie Upravlenie SSSR, *Chislennost' i sostav naseleniia SSSR*, p. 362.

[4] Saidbaev, *Islam i obshchestvo*, pp. 144-45, 204-5, 222, 225; G. Oymahmadov, "Ba"ze mas"alhoi amali gardonidani islohoti maktabhoi ma"lumoti umumi va kasbi dar respublika," *Kommunisti Tojikiston*, September 1985, p. 55; Ahmadov, "Talaboti khojagii khalqi," p. 70; A. Sattorov, "Deha simoi shahr," p. 2; Fedorova, *Goroda Tadzhikistana*, pp. 16, 26-27.

[5] A. V. Kozenko and L. F. Monogarov, "Statisticheskoe izuchenie pokazateli odnonatsional'noi i smeshannoi brachnosti v Dushanbe," *Sovetskaia etnografiia*, no. 6 (1971), pp. 113, 116-18; L. M. Drobizheva, "Kul'tura i mezhnatsional'nye otnosheniia v SSSR," *Voprosy istorii*, 1979, no. 11 (November), p. 8; Saidbaev, *Islam i obshchestvo*, p. 222.

[6] Jabborova, "Ba"ze problemahoi," p. 88.

immoral.[7] Soviet sources testify to the weight of this opinion in compelling people of Muslim background, regardless of personal religious convictions, to observe Islamic rituals and norms of conduct.[8]

Islam and National Identity. Soviet authorities have complained about the close association between Islam and the national identity of Soviet Muslims since the 1960s. Then, as in the 1970s and 1980s, the central theme on the propaganda level is the benefit to Islam from this linkage: Islam remains influential because its leaders present Islamic rites as national ones, and secular national ones as religious.[9] Some Soviet commentators blame the problem largely on the activities of the mullahs who actively promote belief in the unity of the Islamic and national heritage to promote their own influence.[10]

Propaganda aside, there is nothing implausible in the idea that Muslim communal leaders, who have learned how to function under restrictive Soviet conditions, should make such an argument; indeed, there is much truth to it. More scholarly Soviet treatments of the subject do not attribute the strong connection between religious and ethnic identity primarily to the mullahs' machinations but recognize that Islam has become an integral part of the outlook and way of life of the faithful while absorbing elements of pre-Islamic traditions. As a result, even non-believers consider Islam to be part of their national heritage.[11] Recent studies made in Tajikistan show that many do not distinguish between being a Muslim and being a Tajik. Put differently, failure to observe major religious rites is perceived as a deviation from national traditions.[12]

The link between religion and national identity is not unique to Islam. For example, the Brezhnev era witnessed the emergence of a number of vocal advocates of the bond between Russian Orthodoxy and Russian nationality. Soviet authorities suppressed the most assertive proponents of this view during the 1970s[13] but did not stage a similar crackdown among Muslims. In the Gorbachev era Russian nationalists have been allowed to operate more openly. It is too soon to tell whether this will evolve into a policy of full-scale tolerance of

[7] Saidbaev, *Islam i obshchestvo*, p. 215; Baimuradov, "Byt' ubezhdennym," p. 21.

[8] E. Dzhuraeva, "Reshitel'noe 'Net!' — predrasudkam," *Agitator Tadzhikistana*, 1981, no. 23 (December), p. 23; Ashirov, *Musul'manskaia propoved'*, p. 43; *Islam v SSSR*, p. 75; Madzhidov, *Osobennosti formirovaniia*, p. 45; Saidbaev, *Islam i obshchestvo*, p. 225.

[9] Khalmukhamedov, "O chem govoriat," p. 59; Radzhabov, "Prichiny sushchestvovanie," p. 17; "Preniia po otchetam Tsentral'nogo Komiteta," *Kommunist Tadzhikistana*, March 4, 1966, p. 4. See also various works by N. Ashirov, the main contemporary propagandist on this subject.

[10] Ashirov, *Musul'manskaia propoved'*, pp. 54, 65; Khashimov, "Religiia i byt," pp. 64-65, 68-69; Boimurodov, "Sotsializmi mutaraqqi," p. 75; Khalmukhamedov, "O chem govoriat," p. 59; and *Islam v SSSR*, pp. 50-51.

[11] Saidbaev, *Islam i obshchestvo*, pp. 5, 216-19; *Islam v SSSR*, pp. 5, 30, 117.

[12] Tagaeva, "Doiti do serdtsa kazhdogo," p. 23; Dadabaeva, "Sama soboi ne otomret," p. 2; idem, "Konkretno-sotsiologicheskie issledovaniia," p. 258; Madzhidov, Osobennosti formirovaniia, p. 45; and *Islam v SSSR*, p. 75.

[13] Dunlop, *The Faces of Contemporary Russian Nationalism*, pp. 50-56.

such people. There is no indication that advocates of the link between Islam and national traditions will also be allowed greater leeway.

The Family. Family influence is another oft-cited cause of Islam's persistence in Central Asia. This is hardly surprising, as it is normal in most societies for the family to have a large role in instilling its values in the next generation. Moreover, in the Soviet Union, where religious proselytizing is illegal, the family has an even more critical role than elsewhere. It is generally accepted that Islamic values and observances learned in childhood become deeply ingrained and a part of the normal routine of life, so that when a child grows up continued adherence will seem appropriate — even if the person is not pious.[14]

This is the case in Tajikistan. A 1984 survey conducted in the Leninobod *oblast'* of northern Tajikistan reported that more than half the respondents had close relatives who were believers, although only a small minority described themselves as believers. Under the conditions of an officially conducted Soviet survey, it is hard to take the latter claim at face value. Even though few admitted to piety, a majority asserted that they participated in religious rituals on the grounds that these constitute family traditions.[15] Another recent survey found that a vast majority of young believers attribute their religiosity to upbringing at home. Indeed, many children have already become religious by the time they start school and, the survey shows, a "significant" portion of them do not become atheists in school, even though instruction in atheism is mandatory. After education ends, the countervailing influences of family and community continue.[16]

Families treat religious books as prized possessions; they are used for teaching the children and for reading aloud. Stories about Sufi *ishans* and saints are thus passed along from generation to generation. A survey of young people on a Tajikistani *kolkhoz* found that those from religious families believe it would upset their elders were they not to pray. Families can pray at home without reliance on a mullah or a special house of worship. Thus families can establish a religious environment for children. Parents also bring children to mosques, especially on religious holidays.[17] Some unofficial mullahs and Sufi adepts follow in their fathers' footsteps.[18]

[14] Saidbaev, *Islam i obshchestvo*, pp. 223-25, 227, 251-52.

[15] Faizibaeva, "Novye obriady," p. 24.

[16] Dadabaeva, "Konkretno-sotsiologicheskie issledovaniia," p. 257.

[17] Komilov, "Ba"ze sababhoi," p. 13; A. Safarov, "Tashakkuli jahonbinii ilmi," p. 94; "Vazhnaia chast'," p. 3; Madzhidov, "Modernistskie tendentsii," p. 239; "Maktab va tarbiyai ateistii khonandagon," *Gazetai Muallimon*, January 17, 1984, p. 4; Jabborova, "Ba"ze problemahoi," p. 88; Yunusov, "Mashvarati muallimoni zabon va adabiyot," p. 55; Dadabaeva, "Konkretno-sotsiologicheskie issledovaniia," p. 257.

[18] A. Safarov, *Boqimondahoi*, p. 13. Sanginov, "Ashki nadomat," p. 4; Rabiev, "V klass ... s koranom?" p.2.

Soviet sources usually portray the family's religious influence on the young as something that happens without regard for the child's preferences, but one Soviet author concedes that some students strongly dislike school efforts to counter the family's influence in religious matters.[19]

Women. Soviet writers admit that women constitute a large part of the Muslim faithful today and try to explain why. The routine answer presumes the existence of a self-perpetuating cycle: women raised in an Islamic environment receive less education, marry young, and become housewives. Therefore, they do not develop the higher level of consciousness of a worker and, consequently, do not become atheists.[20]

There is some truth to this greatly oversimplified explanation. Women in Tajikistan do receive less education than men. Women belonging to the indigenous nationalities account for only 44 percent of the total number of women employed outside the home in Tajikistan and 38.2 percent of those employed in industry.[21] Employment opportunities are limited, for although some factories have established branches in rural areas, the number remains small.[22] Nonetheless, they are employed. In 1981 women accounted for 52 percent of the *kolkhoz* labor force, and served mostly as low-level or unskilled laborers. Many women cultivate the private garden plots allowed *kolkhoz* members, an important economic activity that enhances the family diet and provides a valuable surplus that can be sold for high prices in urban markets.[23] Women's employment in garden plot cultivation is common in many agricultural regions of the Soviet Union.

Were women to stay longer in school, they would not necessarily work in industry. Vocational education in Tajikistan is concentrated in cities; what is available in villages tends to be of severely restricted choice and low quality.[24] Some rural families that might allow some departure from tradition and let a daughter pursue vocational education may be deterred by the absence of nearby vocational schools

[19] Komilov, "Ba"ze sababhoi," p. 12.

[20] Dadabaeva, "Nastoichivost', nastupatel'nost', planomernost'," *Kommunist Tadzhikistana*, October 27, 1981, p. 2; "Vospitanie ateistov," *Agitator Tadzhikistana*, 1980, no. 9 (May), p. 24; Ahmadov, "San"at va tashakkuli jahonbinii ilmii," p. 94; N. Safarov, "Tarbiyai ateisti," p. 2; Zikriyoeva, "Komsomol i ateisticheskoi vospitanie devushek," p. 19.

[21] Madzhidov, *Osobennosti formirovaniia*, pp. 46-47; Oqilova, "Fa"oli sotsialii," pp. 45-46.

[22] Dadabaeva, "Konkretno-sotsiologicheskie issledovaniia," pp. 254-55

[23] Oqilova, "Fa"oli sotsialii zanoni Tojikiston," pp. 46-48; S. Mirzoshoev, "Rasmu oinhoi nav va tarbiyai ateisti," *Tojikistoni Soveti*, April 16, 1985, p. 2; V. Vyborova, "Tafovothoi sotsialii territoriali va rohhoi bartaraf kardani onho," *Kommunisti Tojikiston*, 1983, no. 9 (September), pp. 38-39; E. Dzhuraeva, "Reshitel'noe 'Net!' — Predrasudkam," *Agitator Tadzhikistana*, 1981, no. 23 (December), pp. 22-23. N. Lubin, *Labour and Nationality in Soviet Central Asia* (Princeton: Princeton University Press, 1984), p. 69.

[24] B. Rasulzoda, "Hunarmand har jo buvad sarfaroz," *Adabiyot va san"at*, July 26, 1984, pp. 3, 5; O. Qurbonbekov, "Zuhuroti navi ghamkhori," *Gazetai muallimon*, February 16, 1984, p. 3; Yu. Yusufbekov, "Tarbiyai mehnati khonandegon," *Gazetai muallimon*, February 28, 1984, pp. 3, 4; Shoismatulloev, "Chorsui zindagi," p. 3.

and the daughter's need to go to a city, where she would live in a dormitory. The authorities encourage girls who learn non-agricultural trades to learn ones that are stereotypically woman's work — cooking, weaving, spinning, sewing, and being a sales clerk.[25]

Muslim women of Tajikistan bear sole responsibility for house-keeping chores, as is the norm throughout the Soviet Union, and, given their high birthrates, are likely to have many children to care for. Day-care facilities, labor-saving appliances, and services are scarce, especially in the countryside. Only 2.6 percent of the republic's day-care centers are located in the villages.[26]

Thus, the notion that Central Asian women are under-employed because they are under-represented in salaried employment ouside the home does not consider their extensive employment in the house-hold. The obstacles to women's employment outside the home are the result not only of Islamic social attitudes but also of the inadequate opportunities for training and employment. It further reflects the Soviet system's failure to alleviate the traditional burden of women's domestic responsibilities, which also remains a problem in the European part of the Soviet Union, where female employment ouside the home is common.

The Mullahs. Soviet sources assert that the mullahs play a role second only to that of the family in ensuring Islam's survival. Indeed, the two act in concert. The mullahs meet people's emotional needs in ways that the secular institutions of Soviet society cannot. They give parents advice on child-rearing, with an emphasis on religious instruction. They also play a generally influential role in family life. They reportedly instruct village children in Islam.[27] References to mullahs indicate that some are itinerant. One unofficial mullah who proselytized extensively in the mid-1980s traveled by automobile through Qurghonteppa province. It is possible that other unofficial mullahs are similarly mobile.[28]

Medicine and Folk Islam. Folk healing is one of the most important functions performed for the general population of believers by Sufis and other representatives of unofficial Islam. The state of health care in Tajikistan is such that folk healers are an attractive, or at least more readily available, source of treatment. There is a

[25] "Mehnat — omili muhimi tashakkuli shakhsiiat," *Gazetai muallimon*, June 2, 1984, p. 2; "Dukhtaroni aziz!," *Tojikistoni Soveti*, April 9, 1985, p. 4. Sh. Shoismatalloev, "Chorsui zindagi," *Adabiyet va san"at*, July 26, 1984, p. 3. Rasulzoda, "Hunarmand har jo buvad sarfaroz," *Adabiyot va san"at*, May 24, 1984, p. 5.

[26] Dadabaeva, "Konkretno-sotsiologieheski issledovaniia," pp. 255-56; Dzhuraeva, "Reshitel'noe 'Net!'" pp. 22-23.

[27] Jabborova, "Ba"ze prolemahoi" p. 88; Komilov, "Ba"ze sababhoi," p. 12; Dadabaeva, "Sama soboi," p. 2; Boimurodov, "Sotsializmi mutaraqqi," p. 77; Saidbaev, *Islam i obshchestvo*, p. 246. Sanginov, "Ashki nadomat," p.4; Rabiev, "V klass . . . s koranom?" p.2.

[28] Rabiev, "Idushchie v nikuda," p.3.

serious shortage of modern medical care in rural areas.[29] Even where modern medical care is available, its employees too often inhabit a separate, unbridgeable world from that of their patients.[30] Language is part of the problem: Tajiks who do not speak Russian or who speak it poorly enter an alien environment when they travel to clinics and hospitals. Some Tajik doctors may be no better able to bridge the linguistic gulf than their non-Tajik colleagues. A Tajik doctor inhabits a different social milieu from that of the vast majority of his fellow Tajiks. To complete his medical training successfully he will have to belong to the roughly 28 percent of the republic's Tajiks who claim to speak Russian as their first or second language (according to the 1979 census). The medical curriculum slights the teaching of the Tajik language. The quality of Tajik-language instruction in the school system as a whole suffers serious defects. Most Tajiks know one of the numerous local dialects, not standard literary Tajik.[31] When a doctor cannot understand a patient's description of symptoms, the problems are obvious. And if a patient does enter a state hospital, his poor morale in a linguistically and culturally alien world can impede his recovery. The gulf between the patient and the health care system is further widened by the rudeness and inattention to which patients are commonly subjected. It is really not surprising that many Muslims prefer folk healers to modern medicine of the Soviet sort.[32]

Foreign Stimuli

Increased Islamic activism outside the Soviet Union, especially in Iran and Afghanistan, has probably caught the attention of some Soviet Muslims, but it is difficult for outsiders to discern the nature of their interest. Rumors abound, but no solid evidence indicates that this influence has increased attention to spiritual matters or stimulated hopes for greater local autonomy or for secession from the USSR.

There is one known instance in which an unofficial mullah, a member of the Wahhabi sect, Abdullo Saidov, advocated the creation of an Islamic state. Revealingly, his plan shows how widely the Soviet-imposed borders have been accepted, for the Islamic state he envisioned was to exist in Tajikistan, not in Central Asia as a whole. On

[29] Dadabaeva, "Konkretno-sotsiologicheskie issledovaniia," p. 256; idem, "Sama soboi," p. 2; *Kommunist Tadzhikistana*, January 26, 1986, p. 3; TadzhikTA, "Pretvorim v zhizn'," p. 3; "Rezoliutsiia XIX s"ezda Kommunisticheskoi Parti Tadzhikistana," *Agitator Tadzhikistana*, 1981, no. 5 (March), p. 14.

[30] M. Tokhirov, "Dukhtur bemor va zabon," *Gazetai muallimon*, September 21, 1985, p. 4.

[31] Ibid; Tsentral'noe Staticheskoe Upravlenie SSR, *Chislennost i sostav naseleniia SSSR* (Moscow, 1984), pp. 132-33; I. M. Oranskii, *Tadzhikoiazychnye etnograficheskie gruppy Gissarskoi doliny (Sredniaia Aziia,* (Moscow, 1983), pp. 29-30; Iu. Akbarov, "Az 'Alifbo' to 'Adabiyot'," *Tojikistoni Soveti*, August 20, 1985, p. 4; A. Mulloev, "Qarzi grazhdani," *Gazetai Muallimon*, June 4, 1987, p. 4.

[32] TadzhikTA, "Pretvorim v zhizn'," p. 4.

one occasion he recommended petitioning the forthcoming Twenty-Seventh Party Congress to establish this Islamic state; on another he made an inflammatory speech to a gathering in one village, stopping just short of an appeal to arms. Saidov has been arrested and imprisoned.[33]

This story came to light in the era of frankness encouraged by Mikhail Gorbachev. It is unusual for the specifics it provides on the influence exerted by religious broadcasting from Islamic countries. There is no comparable evidence to indicate whether there were earlier incidents of this type which were not reported in the pre-*glasnost'* era. We also do not know whether domestic Soviet Muslim interest has changed through 1980-88, as armed resistance to the Soviet invasion of Afghanistan persisted. Nor do we know how Soviet Muslims regard the Islamic government in Iran, with its bloody, internecine power struggles, stalemated reforms, and prolonged, costly war with Iraq.

The Soviet Complaint. The Soviets have complained repeatedly about foreign broadcasts on Islamic themes, as the following commentary shows:

In this struggle of ideas [between socialism and imperialism], the Islamic religion occupies a special place because class enemies either of the West or of the East, using various means — radio, television, the press, books, tourism, etc. — wish to exert their influence under the banner of Islam or at least its revolution.[34]

However, such assertions do not reveal how extensively Iranian or Afghanistani Muslims have influenced their co-religionists in Soviet Central Asia. The Soviets highlight foreign influences to divert attention from domestic conditions that contribute to Islam's persistence. This concern over foreign religious propaganda is not limited to Islam. In recent years the Soviets have also complained about Christian themes in broadcasts aimed at European parts of the country.[35]

Moreover, a long-standing theme of Soviet domestic propaganda in general is that the country is engaged in an intense struggle against foreign enemies, led by the main "imperialist powers," who wish to destroy everything that the Soviet Union has achieved.[36]

[33] Rabiev, "Idushchie v nikuda," p. 3.

[34] M. Davlatov, "Modernizatsiyai kontseptsiyahoi ijtimoiyu siyosii islomi hozira," *Kommunisti Tojikiston*, 1985, no. 6 (June) p. 81. For other expressions of this theme, see also Jabborova, "Ba"ze problemahoi," p. 87; Komilov,"Omili mu himi," p. 24; *Kommunist Tadzhikistana*, January 26, 1986, p. 3; and Vagabov, *Islam i voprosy*, pp. 76-77.

[35] "Aktual'nye voprosy ideologicheskoi, massovo-politicheskoi raboty partii," p. 24; A. Lasevich, "Religiia i sovremennaia ideologicheskaia bor'ba," *Kommunist Belorussii*, 1983, no. 3, pp. 73, 75-76; *Diversiia v efire* (Moscow: Novosti, 1980).

[36] One example of this widespread theme in Soviet sources is Konstantin Chernenko's June 15, 1983, address to the Plenum of the Central Committee of the CPSU, which was devoted to ideological issues. "Aktual' nye voprosy ideologicheskoi, massovo-politicheskoi raboty partii," *Agitator Tadzhikistana*, 1983, no. 14 (July), pp. 13, 21.

Stimuli from Western and Pro-Western Sources. The Soviets are concerned about Islamic propaganda from Western countries as well as from the Middle East. One Soviet treatment of Islam aimed at a mass audience devotes a full chapter to the way the United States has long used Islam to further its "imperialist" designs.[37] According to this argument, Western propaganda about Islam tries to drive a wedge between Muslim states and the Soviet Union, which has their interests at heart, and also foments nationalist-religious tensions among the peoples of the Soviet Union. The upsurge of Islamic activism outside the Soviet Union since the late 1970s has heightened the imperialists' awareness of Islam as a political force.[38]

Soviet commentators react more strongly to radio broadcasts about Islam from non-Muslim countries than to those from Islamic countries.[39] Much of the criticism of foreign propaganda aimed at Soviet Muslims, including on Pan-Islamic and Pan-Turkic themes, is directed against non-Muslim scholars and Western organizations.[40] When the Soviets identify Muslims as the source of hostile propaganda about Islam, the targets of criticism are usually not the Afghans or Iranians but actors at a further remove, such as Pakistan, Qatar, and Egypt. Saudi Arabia is singled out because of its financial support for the Afghan resistance, its critique of Islam's status in the Soviet Union, and the anti-Soviet activities of the Mecca-based World Islamic League. A small number of Soviet Muslim emigrés in Europe and the Middle East who publicly criticize Soviet policy toward Muslim citizens are occasionally denounced; the prime target is Baymirza Hayit, a writer from Central Asia who fought the Soviets during World War II, and now lives in West Germany.[41]

Afghanistan and Iran. The Soviet Union has not been able to seal its border with Iran and Afghanistan as tightly as it would wish. Borderguards, under the authority of the KGB, and the customs service are both supposed to prevent illicit traffic across Central Asia's southern border. Yet the border's permeability was illustrated dra-

[37] Akhmedov, *Islam*, chap. 2; also pp. 3-4.

[38] U. Sharifov, "Butoni ideologhoi bourzhuazi dar borai vaz''i islom dar SSSR," *Kommunisti Tojikiston*, 1985, no. 8 (August), pp. 73-74, 77; S. Islomov, "Beasosii tahrifi bourzhuazii taraqqiyoti sotsialiyu iqtisodii respublikahoi Osiyoi Miyona," *Kommunisti Tojikiston*, 1985, no. 6 (June), p. 88; Vagabov, *Islam i voprosy*, pp. 112-13; *Islam v SSSR*, pp. 120-21; S. Nikishov, "Opiraias' na Leninskoe ateisticheskoe nasledie," *Agitator Tadzhikistana*, 1980, no. 15 (August), p. 15; Iurkov, "Pod pritselom SShA," p. 30; Sh. Abdulloev, " 'Sofkorii' jahonbini chist?" *Tojikistoni Soveti*, June 8, 1985, p. 3.

[39] A typical listing of stations criticized is Voice of America, the BBC, Deutsche Welle, Radio Liberty, Radio Free Europe, Radio Israel, and Radio Beijing. See S. Hasanova, "Du jahon — du tarzi hayot," *Kommunisti Tojikiston*, 1985, no. 2 (February), p. 49.

[40] S. Safarov, "Propaganda naoborot," *Komsomolets Tadzhikistana*, June 16, 1985, p. 3; Akhmedov, *Islam*, pp. 117ff.; Sharifov, "Butoni ideologhoi," p. 74.

[41] Sharifov, "Butoni ideologhoi," p. 74; Abdulloev, "'Sofkorii' jahonbini chist?" p. 3; Davlatov, "Modernizatsiyai kontseptsiyahoi," p. 81; Kh. Ismailov, "Otvet proritsateliam," *Nauka i religiia*, 1980, no. 1, pp. 42-43; *Islam v SSSR*, pp. 156-58, 160-61. Sanginov, "Ashki nadomat," p. 4.

matically in March and April 1987, when Afghan guerrillas (two different groups have claimed responsibility) staged two cross-border attacks on southern Tajikistan, specifically the *oblasts* of Kulob and Qurghonteppa. The March attack involved firing across the border, the April attack may have taken the same form or may have included a brief incursion by guerrillas on Soviet soil. The direct military consequences of these small-scale attacks are negligible, except for the harsh reprisals rumored to have been launched by the Soviets against several villages on the Afghan side of the border. There is no reliable information on how the incidents affected the attitudes of Tajikistan's inhabitants. One Tajikistani mass-media account, casting the raids in the most negative light possible, described attacks by foreign enemies directed against civilians as well as border guards.[42]

Smuggling, both from Iran and Afghanistan, is probably a more serious potential influence on Central Asians' attitudes than the guerrilla raids. The Soviet authorities are sufficiently concerned about smuggling that in 1986 they transferred the customs service from the jurisdiction of the foreign trade administration (*Vneshtorg*) to direct accountability to the Council of Ministers. Much of what is smuggled has no direct political significance — consumer goods and drugs — but other items could have — Qur'ans, religious propaganda from Iran (especially in the Turkmen republic) and the Afghanistani guerrillas, and small weapons.[43]

Given the scarcity of Qur'ans in the Soviet Union, a copy may be valued in the ordinary observance of Islam, and not necessarily as part of a new militance. We do not know how the overwhelmingly Sunni Muslims of Central Asia react to Iran's militantly Shi'i propaganda. The Afghan guerrillas are organized into several different groups with different concepts of the place of Islam in society and politics.[44] We do not know how much propaganda, representing which groups' opinions, is smuggled into Central Asia or what Central Asians think of that propaganda.

The Iranian government set up Radio Gorgan to spread its message of fundamentalist Islam to Central Asia.[45] Pakistani broadcasting on Islamic topics can also be heard in Tajikistan. The mullah from Qurghonteppa who advocated the creation of an Islamic state was said to have been influenced by radio broadcasts from both these

[42] *The Washington Post*, April 13, 1987 and April 19, 1987; V. Petkel', "Farzandi Pol'sha — Qahramoni Tojikiston," *Tojikistoni Soveti*, June 13, 1987, p.3.

[43] V. Mitrokhin, "Na tamozhne: proezdom i postoianno," *Iunost'* (Ashkhabad), 1987, no. 7, pp. 43-45; "60th Anniversary of KGB in Turkmen SSR Noted," Joint Publications Research Service, *Soviet Union Political and Sociological*, JPRS-UPS-84-024 (March 22, 1985), p. 98; "Russians open up border to Turkoman and Tartar," *The Sunday Times*, September 11, 1983.

[44] M. N. Shahrani, "Introduction: Marxist 'Revolution' and Islamic Resistance in Afghanistan," *Revolutions and Rebellions in Afghanistan*, pp. 45-49.

[45] Davlatov, "Modernizatsiyai kontseptsiyahoi," p. 81; *Turkmenskaia iskra*, June 15, 1980, p. 3.

countries.[46] The specific messages of such broadcasts must often be contradictory, since the Iranian and Pakistani regimes espouse sharply different interpretations of Islam. On very basic matters, however, the spiritual superiority of Islam and the evils of atheism, for example, they may reinforce each other.

The Communist Party of Tajikistan has expressed concern that the mullahs' powerful role in Iran might inspire imitation by the Muslim leaders in the southern *oblast'* of Kulob. However, the official rhetoric does not reveal actual Iranian influence as opposed to its potential and the need to prevent it by more vigorous atheist propaganda and surveillance.[47]

Soviet discussions about Islam and atheism in Tajikistan between 1979 and early 1986 show no special emphasis on the area closest to Afghanistan. Not every reference specifies a particular part of the republic, nor was every reference found, of course, but the ninety-three geographically specific accounts provide an approximate guide to what the authorities believe deserves attention. Tajikistan can be divided into four zones: Leninobod *oblast'* in the north; a central zone around Dushanbe; Qurghonteppa and Kulob *oblast's* in the south, bordering Afghanistan; and the sparsely populated Gorno-Badakhshan Autonomous *Oblast'* in the southeast, bordering Afghanistan and China. Religious and atheist issues arose twice as often in writing with reference to the north and center of the republic as in the south and southeast combined.[48] This is despite the fact that the, Hisor (Gissar) Mountains, an east-west chain lying north of Dushanbe, probably interferes with radio reception from Iran.

There has been curiosity in the West about the possibility that the Soviet military presence in Afghanistan has stimulated discontent among Soviet Muslims. It is quite possible that some of them disapprove of the war but little is known about the expression of their discontent. In any case, opposition to the war is motivated by considerations other than Islamic solidarity. Reports tell of Ukrainians, Balts, Georgians, and Armenians who also disapprove of the war.[49] Some Soviet Muslims serving in Afghanistan are reported to have defected, but their numbers appear to be small. Non-Muslim Soviet citizens have also defected or emigrated in recent years. In the opinion of Olivier Roy, a French anthropologist who has closely followed the war in Afghanistan, there are "few politically motivated deserters [from the Soviet forces in Afghanistan], but increasing numbers of

[46] Sanginov, "Ashki nadomat," p. 4.

[47] Tagaeva, "Doiti do serdtsa kazhdogo," p. 24.

[48] There were thirty-four references to Leninobod *oblast'* or its components, twenty-eight to the components of the central zone, fourteen to Qurghonteppa *oblast'* and its components, thirteen to Kulob *oblast'* and its components, and four to Gorno-Badakhshan.

[49] U.S. Department of State, Bureau of Intelligence and Research, "Public Support for Afghan War Lower in Republics," *Soviet Nationalities Survey*, February 1986, pp. 1-2.

Soviet soldiers, sometimes drug addicts, have been abandoning their posts or allowing themselves to be captured."[50]

Some observers contend that Soviet Muslim troops were withdrawn from Afghanistan soon after the invasion because their loyalty was questionable. The reports of unreliability are unverifiable. There may be an alternate explanation that has nothing to do with reliability: the initial Soviet invasion force was composed of troops regularly stationed in the military districts nearest Afghanistan, supplemented by local reserves, and therefore included a disproportionate number of Central Asians. Later, regular units replaced the reserves, and, as a result, the troops in Afghanistan reflected the standard ethnic composition of Soviet troops. This would follow an established Soviet pattern; for example, local reserves from western border districts were sent several times into Eastern Europe. Further, Soviet authorities do not act as though they fear for the loyalty of the Central Asian Muslims who have contact with Afghans. The Soviet military continues to draw on troops from Central Asia, including Tajikistan, for operations in Afghanistan.[51]

Tajiks and other Central Asians are used to having influence over Afghans. Central Asians fill many positions in Afghanistan's administration and educational system. For example, several Tajik academics, including some from the State University and the Pedagogical Institute in Dushanbe, work in Kabul.[52] Groups of performing artists have also been sent to Afghanistan since 1979.[53] A delegation of official Tajikistani mullahs has visited Afghanistan. In October 1985, a high-ranking secular delegation visited to observe Tajikistan SSR-Afghanistan Friendship Days.[54]

Delegations from Afghanistan, including members of the government and other supporters of the communist regime, have repeatedly visited Tajikistan, where they were shown factories, farms, schools, and, on at least one occasion in 1986, a mosque.[55] Young Afghans are brought to Dushanbe to study in technical schools and

[50] O. Roy, "Soviets in Danger of Over-extending Themselves," *Manchester Guardian Weekly*, December 25, 1983, p. 14. For a similar view, see also E. R. Girardet, *Afghanistan* (New York: St. Martin's Press, 1985), p. 230.

[51] E. Jones, *Red Army and Society* (Boston: Allen and Unwin, 1985), p. 195; Girardet, *Afghanistan*, pp. 30, 236.

[52] E. Girardet, "Three Years After the Invasion: the Soviet Union's Two-edged Sword in Afghanistan," *The Christian Science Monitor*, December 22, 1982; idem., *Afghanistan*, pp. 144-45; Usmonov, "Inqilob oftobro monad . . . ," p. 3.

[53] "Kontserhoi dusti," *Tojikistoni Soveti*, April 26, 1985, p. 3; "Safar ba kishvari dust," *Tojikistoni Soveti*, October 27, 1985, p. 4; "San"atkoroni tojik dar Afghoniston," *Adabiyot va san"at*, October 31, 1985, p. 15.

[54] Sharifov, "Butoni ideologhoi," p. 77; Tass, "Ruzhoi dustii Ittifoqi Soveti dar Afghoniston," *Adabiyot va san"at*, October 31, 1985.

[55] TadzhikTA, "Vizit Afganskikh druzei," *Kommunist Tadzhikistana*, March 26, 1986, p. 2; *Agitator Tadzhikistana*, 1985, no. 14 (July), p. 32; TadzhikTA, "Hayati vakiloni Afghoniston dar Tojikiston," *Tojikistoni Soveti*, September 22, 1985, p. 3; TadzhikTA, "Mehmonon az Afghoniston," *Tojikistoni Soveti*, October 23, 1985, p. 3.

institutions of higher education.[56] Soviet authorities use the cultural similarities between Tajiks of the USSR and the Persian-speakers of Afghanistan to influence the latter. B. Gh. Ghafurov's history of the Tajiks, *Tojikon*, was published in Kabul in a large Dari (Kabul Persian) edition in 1985 and contained an introduction by Babrak Karmal, then the head of the People's Democratic Party of Afghanistan.[57] A member of the faculty of Tajikistan State University published a book on Dari literature intended for Afghan teachers and students of this subject.[58]

Some see Soviet references since 1979 to the Basmachi as indicative of the authorities' concern (either pre-emptive or reactive) about the impact on Soviet Muslims of Islam's role in the fight against communist rule in Afghanistan. In this view, post-1979 references to the Basmachi represent a dramatic new development, because "in the past, discussion of the Basmachi has been, with few exceptions, more or less taboo."[59] In fact, the topic was by no means taboo in the period between the end of World War II and 1979. In Tajikistan, several novels, at least one film, an opera, and a ballet about the Basmachi were produced during this period.[60] A Tajik history textbook published in 1965 discussed the Basmachi in terms much like those used now, including that the Basmachi were reactionaries backed by foreign imperialists. On the all-Union level, a major study of the subject appeared in 1976.[61] The first edition of Saidbaev's *Islam i obshchestvo*, arguably the most important Soviet study of domestic Islam published in the 1970s, discussed the Basmachi without treating them like an especially sensitive topic.[62]

At the same time, discussion of the Basmachi has increased since 1979 and Soviet domestic propaganda about Afghanistan explicitly associates anti-communist guerrillas there with the Basmachi. It as-

[56] O. B. Karimova, "Muvaffaqiyathoi maorifi khalqi mo namunai ibrat baroi mamlakathoi Osiyo va Afrika," *Maktabi Soveti*, 1982, no. 10 (October), p. 7; M. Tabibulloeva, "Tashkiloti partiyavi va tarbiyai mutakhassisoni javon," *Kommunisti Tojikiston*, 1982, no. 11 (November), pp. 68, 70; TadzhikTA, "Laureathoi festival'," *Tojikistoni Soveti*, March 28, 1985, p. 4; A. Yuldasheva, "Vokhuri internatsionaliston," *Gazetai Muallimon*, June 29, 1985, p. 1; G. Mirzoeva, "Bazmi dusti," *Adabiyot va san''at*, December 6, 1984, p. 11; G. Uzbekov, "Jon ravshan as furughi dusti," *Gazetai Muallimon*, May 1, 1986, p. 2; J. Hotamov, "Bakhshida ba Falastin," *Tojikistoni Soveti*, May 21, 1986, p. 4.

[57] A. Latifov and A. Rabiev, "Dar nisbati Khujand va farzandon ash," *Tojikistoni Soveti*, September 25, 1985, p. 3; I. Usmonov, "Inqilob oftobro monad . . ." *Tojikistoni Soveti*, April 27, 1986, p. 3.

[58] The book is *Nigarshe be nasri muosiri darii Afghoniston* by Kh. Asoev. See F. Najmonov, "Rahovardi khub," *Sadoi Sharq*, 1984, no. 7, pp. 131, 133.

[59] Bennigsen, "Soviet Islam," p. 69.

[60] *Istoriia kul'turnogo stroitel'stva v Tadzhikistane 1917-1977 gg.*, vol. 2 (Dushanbe: Donish, 1983), pp. 179, 258; T. Rakowska-Harmstone, *Russia and Nationalism in Central Asia* (Baltimore: Johns Hopkins University Press, 1970), pp. 256, 258, 260.

[61] N. Pak and U. Pulodov, "Tarikhi khalq," *Sadoi Sharq*, 1984, no. 9, pp. 133-34; Iu. A. Poliakov and A. I. Chugunov, *Konets basmachestva* (Moscow: Nauka, 1976).

[62] Saidbaev, *Islam i obshchestvo*, 1st ed. (Moscow: Nauka, 1978), pp. 131, 139, and passim. The book cleared censorship in June 1978, before the emergence of extensive anti-communist resistance in Afghanistan.

serts that the Afghan guerrillas, like the Basmachi, are counterrevolutionary marauders who share no interests with ordinary Afghan citizens. Their support comes from imperialists, though they pretend to act in the name of Islam. Most important of all, recalling that the Basmachi lost reminds Soviet citizens that Moscow won and suggests that it will win again.[63]

Propaganda within the USSR argues that support for the "counterrevolutionaries" in Afghanistan comes only from reactionaries; it is alleged that most believers, including most mullahs, support the new order. According to this argument, it is only the counterrevolutionaries who have killed Muslims, including more than a hundred mullahs. They also are accused of various acts of sacrilege. The government of Hafizollah Amin, which followed a heavy-handed anti-Islamic policy, is criticized in Soviet propaganda for playing into the hands of the counterrevolutionaries. Babrak Karmal gets credit for ending these objectionable measures and reassuring Muslims that the revolution does not threaten their religious beliefs. The Soviet authorities reprinted Karmal's March 14, 1982, address to the national conference of the People's Democratic Party of Afghanistan. In it, he repeatedly stated that Muslims are free to practice their religion, that patriotic mullahs support the revolution, and that there need be no conflict between Islam and revolution. Soviet rhetoric also blames imperialists and Afghan reactionaries for conducting a deceptive campaign to present themselves as defenders of Islam.[64]While Soviet Muslims may or may not believe such propaganda, it shows something about the Soviet authorities' views. They see the international attention to Islam's political influence in Afghanistan as a potentially worrisome matter. Accordingly, they are making strenuous efforts to prevent Soviet citizens from seeing the issue as one of Islam vs. communism.

But the Soviet authorities also see some positive effects of militant Islam. The keystone of the Soviet line on this subject since 1981 is Leonid Brezhnev's pronouncement at the Twenty-Sixth Party Congress: the increased political activism of Islam since the late 1970s can be good or bad, depending on the circumstances.

The liberation struggle may unfold under the banner of Islam. The experience of history, including the most recent, bears witness to that. However, it also shows that

[63] R. Masov, "Basmachestvo. Uroki istorii," *Kommunist Tadzhikistana,* January 13, 1982, p. 2; V. Artemov, "Pravda i vymysly ob aprel'skoi revoliutsii v Afganistane," *Agitator Tadzhikistana,* 1982, no. 23 (December), p. 29.

[64] L. Kurochkina, "Afganistan: vremia peremen," *Agitator Tadzhikistana,* 1980, no. 12 (June), pp. 31-32; L. Sheshnev, "Terror protiv afganskogo naroda," *Agitator Tadzhikistana,* 1986, no. 2 (January), pp. 28-30; V. Basov, "Postup' afganskoi revoliutsii," *Agitator Tadzhikistana,* 1985, no 18 (September), p. 30; B. Karmal, "O proekte programmy deistvii NDPA i zadachakh po ukrepleniiu partii i usileniiu ee sviazei s narodom," *Kommunist,* 1982, no. 5 (March), pp. 97, 98-99, 102; *Islam v SSSR,* pp. 153, 163; "Kto podnimaet," p. 2.

reaction operates with Islamic slogans, stirring up counterrevolutionary rebellions. Therefore, the key issue is what is the real content of one movement or another.[65]

The assessment of Islam abroad presented to a mass domestic audience includes much that is positive. This would be inconceivable were the authorities looking at Islamic activism only as a dangerous influence on Soviet Muslims. The message conveyed to Soviet Muslims is clear: Islam can play a progressive role in various foreign countries, not only in those that are socialist oriented, where the leaders can use Islamic rhetoric to mobilize mass support for their reforms. It can serve as a mass ideology espousing many of the things Soviets favor: anti-imperialism (including anti-Americanism and anti-Zionism), rejection of Western economic models, and profound social transformation.[66] The same opinions are voiced by leading Soviet specialists on Islam abroad.[67]

The rise to power of fundamentalist Muslims in Iran and the *jihad* against communist rule in Afghanistan have galvanized opinion among a significant fraction of Muslims in many countries. An important part of the appeal lies in the hope that Islam's social teachings can provide a remedy to the painful disruption of society resulting from Western-inspired (whether liberal or Marxist) programs of change. The new Islamic politics of opposition offers a means to repudiate the domestic political elites (whether capitalist or socialist) while giving its followers the satisfaction of asserting the worth of their heritage after a long period of defensiveness in the face of the obvious strengths of the great powers.

Not many Soviet Muslims are likely to look to Islamic activism for the remedy to their dissatisfactions with the Soviet system. Some have benefited from the Soviet version of affirmative action and have a stake in preserving the system. Educated Central Asians are likely to be deterred from Iran's way by watching that country's evolution since 1979, especially the mullahs' seizure of power. The downfall of Mehdi Bazargan, Abol Hasan Bani Sadr, Sadeq Qotbzadeh, and others does not augur well for the fate of educated Soviet Central Asians under a militant Islamic regime.

Influence from abroad has strikingly little importance in Tajikistan; rather, domestic conditions are key to understanding the con-

[65] *Pravda*, February 24, 1981, p. 3. This view has been widely disseminated in the Soviet Union among the general populace as well as in political and scholarly circles. See, e.g., Davlatov, "Modernizatsiayi kontseptsiyahoi," p. 82.

[66] Iurkov, "Pod pretselom SShA," p. 31; S. Safarov, "Propaganda naobarot," *Komsomolets Tadzhikistana*, June 16, 1985, p. 3; Aliev, "Islam i sovremennost'," pp. 20, 22; G. M. Kerimov, "Pod zelenym znamenem islama," *Kommunist Tadzhikistana*, November 13, 1980, p. 3.

[67] Atkin, "Soviet Attitudes," pp. 283-84, 286-92; B. G. Kapustin, "Osnovye napravleniia istoricheskoi evoliutsii sotsial'nykh islamskikh uchenii," Akademiia Nauk SSSR, Institut Vostokovendeniia, *Islam: problemy ideologii prava, politiki i ekonomiki* (Moscow: Nauka, Glavnaia redaktsiia Vostochnoi literatury, 1985), pp. 33-34, 37-38; L. R. Polonskaia, "Sovremennye musul'manskie ideinye techeniia," *Islam: problemy*, pp. 13, 15, 17, 20, 22-23.

tinued influence of Islam. This is confirmed by the behavior of Soviet authorities in Tajikistan, who dislike foreign influences but treat domestic causes as far more pervasive and significant.

Soviet Policy
toward Domestic Islam

Soviet officials do not passively observe the persistence of Islam within the USSR but pursue a number of policies to keep Islam's influence within manageable limits and reduce it if possible. Such policies began long before the recent wave of international Islamic political activity began.

Proselytizing Atheism

The regime uses its control of education and the media to steer its population toward atheism. Soviet law ostensibly grants equal rights to religious believers and atheists, with the significant difference that atheist proselytizing is official policy while there is no legal protection for religious proselytizing. It is also illegal for children to participate in religious ceremonies. However, the situation in Tajikistan shows that enforcement of this regulation is far from complete.

An Institute of Scientific Atheism was established in 1964 as part of the Academy of Social Sciences of the Central Committee of the CPSU. It serves as a center for research on religious and atheist topics and for the dissemination of information on methods of atheist proselytizing. Similar functions within Tajikistan are performed by the republic's House of Scientific Atheism, which began operations in 1972 and has branches on the *oblast'* level.[1] The republic's Academy of Sciences has added a new component (apparently during the Brezhnev era), the Sector of the History of Religion and Atheism, which is a part of the Division of Philosophy. This sector studies attitudes toward religion and the reasons for the persistence of religion.[2] Tajikistan State University offers a graduate degree in the history, theory, and practice of atheism. Between 1965 and 1980, twenty people wrote dissertations on atheist topics, two of them at the doctoral level, the rest at the candidate level.[3] In the early 1980s

---

[1] *Islam v SSSR*, p. 142.

[2] Madzhidov, "Vospityvat' ubezhdennykh ateistov," p. 26; Baimurodov, *Leninskii printsip*, pp. 81-82.

[3] The degree of candidate of sciences is comparable to an American doctorate. The Soviet doctorate requires years of work in the profession and the writing of a monograph (beyond the dissertation written for the candidate's degree).

there were ten additional candidate-level dissertations in this general field. Of twelve doctoral dissertations on atheist subjects defended between 1978 and 1980, just less than half pertained to Islam.[4]

The key Soviet propaganda organization dealing with matters of religion and atheism is the Znanie (knowledge) Society, established in 1947. Znanie Societies primarily conduct lectures, publish propaganda tracts, and hold conferences. Tajikistan, like other republics of the USSR, has its own Znanie Society, which claimed almost 28,000 members by 1977; it also has organizations in the four *oblast*'s, fifty organizations in cities and towns, and 1,600 organizations in the *raions*.[5] There are no independent estimates to corroborate these claims. Even if the Znanie Society's strength on paper approximates the official numbers, many local organizations do not actually function. Almost anyone with an education or whose work involves social mobilization, including teachers and doctors, is encouraged to join, especially in the countryside; many of them are likely to be strictly nominal members. Those members who are more active may be motivated by conviction or by a desire to gain favor with the authorities.

The authorities regard Islam's strength as a problem of manageable proportions rather than a crisis that demands an all-out effort. While the party frequently calls for more and better atheist propaganda, it also recognizes that too vigorous a campaign against Islam would be counterproductive. Furthermore, the prevailing Soviet line is that religion (and especially Islam) is deeply entrenched in the popular consciousness. Therefore, there is no reason to expect it to disappear rapidly, despite the many changes in society wrought by communist rule. Rather, it will disappear gradually.[6] Offending believers (by mocking Islam or emphasizing criticism of Islam over the attractions of atheism) or trying to ban widely observed rites is ineffective and un-Leninist, say the critics of that approach. It can be interpreted as persecution and can even strengthen opposition, as was the case during the Civil War from 1918 through the mid-1920s.[7] These warnings are sufficiently numerous to raise the suspicion that routine atheist propaganda displays precisely the aggressive insensitivity that the critics decry.

Soviet atheist propaganda also contends that Muslims do not have to choose between their faith and the Soviet system because

[4] *Islam v SSSR*, p. 140.

[5] Shukurov, *Kul'turnaia zhizn'*, p. 161.

[6] Vagabov, *Islam i voprosy*, pp. 102-3, 105; Boimurodov, "Sotsializmi mutaraqqi," p. 74; Komilov, "Propagandai ateisti," p. 77.

[7] Baimurodov, "Leninskii printsip," pp. 85-89; Nikishov, "Opiraias'," p. 16; Iu. Chukovenkov, "Individual'naia ateisticheskaia rabota," *Agitator Tadzhikistana*, 1982, no. 8 (April), p. 11; M. Tabarov, "Antireligioznaia rabota po mestu zhitel'stva," *Agitator Tadzhikistana*, 1982, no. 15 (August), p. 17; Komilov, "Propagandai ateisti" p. 75; Saidbaev, *Islam i obshchestvo*, p. 142.

religion has become a "matter of personal conscience, [which] influences only the sphere of personal life" and does not interfere with the rights and duties of citizenship.[8] The message here is that believers can successfully combine some religious views with scientific and socialist principles; they can be fully integrated into Soviet life and participate in the building of a new order.[9] The party seeks to play down the possibility of unrest among Soviet Muslims, especially in response to stimuli from abroad, and seeks also to ensure that atheist propaganda does not antagonize Muslims by impugning their good citizenship.[10]

The Case of Tajikistan

Soviet Efforts. Information about techniques and themes of atheist propaganda is disseminated through the arts and the mass media, including *Agitator Tadzhikistana*, a semi-monthly magazine published in identical Russian and Tajik versions for those who conduct propaganda among the general population (mass propagandists). Books and pamphlets also address religious issues; there has been a modest increase in the number of these published in the Tajik language since the late 1970s.[11] The most significant publication in recent years is the first atheist dictionary in Tajik. It contains lengthy articles on Islamic subjects, in addition to entries on other religions. Topics covered include Sunni and Shi'i Islam, Sufism, and Islamic socialism. However, some subjects are omitted, including several pertinent to Sufism ("asceticism," "order," "divine truth," "mystical union with God," and "eternity") while other subjects receive only cursory treatment, including *ishans* and *jihad* (holy war).[12]

Another vehicle for spreading information about how to promote atheism is the conference, held either at the republican or the local levels. The most important conference of recent years met in Dushanbe on March 26 and 27, 1982, and included party and state officials, scholars, and propagandists from Central Asia, Moscow, and other Soviet regions.[13]

Tajikistan has a large corps of people who engage in atheist propaganda either as their primary activity or as an adjunct to their work in other fields, such as medicine or teaching. In 1982 the re-

[8] Saidbaev, *Islam i obshchestvo*, pp. 201, 216; A. Safarov, "Tashakkuli jahonbinii ilmi," p. 93.

[9] Khalmukhamedov, "O chem govoriat," p. 57; Akhmedov, *Sotsial'naia doktrina islama*, pp. 121, 131-32; Ashirov, *Musul'manskaia propoved'* pp. 30, 63.

[10] Baimurodov, *Leninskii printsip*, pp. 90-91.

[11] Ibid., p. 82.

[12] V. Sharifov and D. Khushkadamov, *Lughati-ma"lumotnomai ateist* (Dushanbe: Irfon, 1985); A. Abdulloev, "Lughatnomai ateist," *Gazetai muallimon*, November 2, 1985, p. 3; S. Sabzoev, "Lughati ateisti ba zaboni tojiki," *Tojikistoni Soveti*, October 18, 1985, p. 4.

[13] R. Madzhidov, "Vospityvat' ubezhdennykh ateistov," p. 26.

public claimed 900 lecturers on atheism.[14] An official of Tajikistan's Znanie Society claimed that some fifteen thousand lectures on atheist topics were given in Tajikistan in the second half of 1979 and throughout 1980.[15] Schools, including "people's universities" (which are not institutions of higher education but numerous local bodies specializing in short propaganda courses) and other organizations at the *oblast'*, city, and *raion* levels, train atheist propagandists. The Central Committee of the Communist Party of Tajikistan periodically holds courses and seminars for the same purpose. Since 1981, Tajikistan has operated schools of "scientific communism," which provide thousands of party and Komsomol members with ideological instruction, including atheism. Party organizations, at least in one *oblast'*, sponsor coordinating councils to handle atheist propaganda.[16]

Komsomol (Communist Youth League) organizations, labor unions, employers, and other institutions are expected to conduct atheist propaganda. Some of these organizations deal primarily or exclusively with women. Foremost among these are the more than 900 women's councils that have been operating in Tajikistan since the early 1980s. Their activities included encouraging women to work in salaried employment outside the home, preventing girls from leaving school early, and curbing Islam's influence on attitudes toward marriage. Clubs exist to conduct lectures among rural women on atheist themes.[17] Schools begun by the Znanie Society in 1976 teach "introductory knowledge of nature, society, and man." Their intended audience is primarily women who have not attended secondary school; the curriculum combines coverage of science and social studies with efforts to discredit religion. By 1981, the seventy-three such schools already established had only about 1,000 students, a minute segment of the population.[18]

Given the key role of schools in the socialization process, it is no surprise that these institutions are expected to instill atheist attitudes in their students. Teachers of all subjects are called on to use their specialties to demonstrate the fallacies of religion. This applies not only to the sciences but also to the social sciences and the humanities. Science classes should explain natural phenomena and debunk miracles. Literature classes should emphasize anti-religious themes in Tajik poetry. History should demonstrate how religion has

[14] *Islam v SSSR*, p. 140.

[15] "Ateisticheskoe vospitanie trudiashchikhsia," *Agitator Tadzhikistana*, 1981, no. 1 (January), p. 28.

[16] Tagaeva, "Doiti do serdtsa kazhdogo," pp. 22-23; Baimurodov, *Leninskii printsip*, p. 82; S. Toshkhujaev, "Maktabi takmili donishhoi siyosi," *Gazetai Muallimon*, April 3, 1984, p. 2.

[17] *Kommunist Tadzhikistana*, January 26, 1986, p. 3; TadzhikTA, "Pretvorim v zhizn'," p. 3.

[18] "Ateisticheskoe vospitanie," p. 28; *Islam v SSSR*, pp. 148-49.

functioned as a reactionary social force and also should provide examples of internal contradictions in religions.[19]

Schools conduct extracurricular atheist propaganda, too. Clubs, films, outings (including trips to holy places), posters, school libraries, lectures, and conferences are intended to convert students to atheism. Schools also are supposed to give lectures to students' parents.[20] Atheist instruction continues in higher and specialized middle education, including a course on the fundamentals of atheism.[21] Dormitories in Dushanbe sponsor lectures and discussion evenings. Sports are used deliberately to fill up young people's spare time and to prevent them from engaging in religious or other "anti-social" activities.[22]

Atheist propaganda in Tajikistan routinely provides scientific explanations for natural phenomena such as earthquakes, floods, and miracles, contrasts modern medicine with folk healing, and inveighs against the role of religion in child-rearing. It also attacks Islam as backward and reactionary (where "reactionary" does not mean opposition to the Soviet regime, but the contention that religions arose in earlier stages of social evolution and are obsolete in the age of socialism). The authorities also target the Ramadan fast, holding the practice to be unhealthful.[23]

The party tries to curtail the influence of religion by introducing secular Soviet rites. These serve both to substitute for religious rites and to celebrate occasions important to the Soviet regime.[24] In addition to secular weddings and funerals, the authorities have tried to spread new rituals for other occasions in the life-cycle: wedding anniversaries, the issuing of a young person's first internal passport, or the start of a youth's term of military service. Patriotic and political holidays, such as May Day, and the anniversaries of the October

[19] J. Mu"minov, "Sukhani tab"i dil," *Tojikistoni Soveti*, May 16, 1985, p. 2; A. Hayotov, "Fizika va tarbiyai ateisti," *Gazetai muallimon*, October 4, 1983, p. 2; A. Sadirov, "Tarbiyai ilmiyo ateistii khonandegon hangomi ta"limi mavzui 'Zaminjunbi'," *Maktabi Soveti*,1982, no. 8 (August), pp. 45-46, 47; Yunusov, "Mashvarati muallimoni zabon va adabiyot," p. 55; A. Mayusufov, "Tarbiyai ateisti dar maktab," *Maktabi Soveti*, 1983, no. 11 (November), p. 7; Komilov, "Omili muhimi," pp. 24-25; G. Mavlonov, "Tarbiyai ateistii talabagon," *Maktabi Soveti*, 1984, no. 4 (April), pp. 28-29; D. Rasulov and M. Sharifkhojaev, "Kruzhoki ta"rikh va roli on dar tarbiyai ateisti khonandegon," *Maktabi Soveti*, 1983, no. 10 (October), pp. 25-26.

[20] M. Gulahmadov, "Tashakkuli jahonbinii marksisti-leninii khonandegon," *Maktabi Soveti*, 1983, no. 3 (October), p. 13; "Maktab va tarbiyai ateistii khonandegon," *Gazetai muallimon*, January 14, 1984, p. 3; "Maktab va tarbiyai ateistii khonandegon," *Gazetai muallimon*, January 17, 1984, p. 4; B. Ismoilov, "Tarbiyai ilmi-ateistii khonandagon dar rafti korhoi berun as sinf," *Maktabi Soveti*, 1983, no. 3 (March), p. 17-18.

[21] Boimurodov, *Leninskii printsip*, pp. 81-82.

[22] V. Vaulin, "Vospitanie ateistov — zadacha kompleksnaia," *Agitator Tadzhikistana*, 1982, no. 12 (June), pp. 25-26.

[23] M. Khojaev and Gh. Nu"monov, "Propagandai ateistiro ta"sirbakhsh menamoem," *Kommunisti Tojikiston*, 1982, no. 10 (October), p. 78; "Maktab va tarbiyai ateistii khonandagon," *Gazetai Muallimon*, January 21, 1984, p. 4; Zikrieeva, "Komsomol i ateisticheskoe vospitanie devushek," p. 20; Mavlonov, "Tarbiyai ateistii talabagon," pp. 28-29; M. Dzhurakulov, "Ateizmu — nastupatel'nost'," *Agitator Tadzhikistana*, 1982, no. 19 (October), p. 25; R. Pulatova, "V bor'be s predrasudkami," *Agitator Tadzhikistana*, June 1980, no. 11 (June), p. 19.

[24] *Kommunist Tadzhikistana*, January 26, 1986, p. 3.

Revolution and victory over Nazi Germany are observed in Tajikistan, as throughout the Soviet Union. This largely agricultural republic also has secular holidays tied to the production of crops, including the Harvest Festival and the Melon and Watermelon Festival. In 1976 Tajikistan's government set the third Sunday in March as the official date for celebrating *No Ruz* (Nav ruz), the Iranian New Year's celebration, traditionally observed on the vernal equinox. The express purpose of the date change was to dissociate the holiday from Islam, a that link evolved during the centuries since Iran's conversion to Islam.[25]

Finally, Soviet authorities can always resort to force in order to curb the influence of Islam. The extremes of Stalinist terror are past, but the state occasionally has used force to thwart what it considered intolerable opposition. A dramatic confrontation occurred in Tashkent in 1969 when a group of Uzbeks attacked Russian spectators at a soccer match. Islam does not seem to have been the issue here, but ethnic animosity certainly was. The fighting was more than the militia could handle, so reinforcements were summoned. After several hours, some fifteen thousand army and militia troops restored order, killing or injuring several dozen people.[26] Should the Soviet leaders ever feel threatened by domestic Islamic militance, there is no reason to doubt that they would use as much force as necessary to eliminate the threat.

Soviet Failure. As with many other aspects of Soviet life, the quality and quantity of anti-religious measures fall far short of the goal. Characteristic problems include drab, routine measures, the excessive criticism of religion (which only alienates believers), and insufficient effort.[27] Organizations that are supposed to proselytize atheist views often slight the subject. Some primary party organizations do nothing at all in this area. People's universities have been criticized on this score, along with clubs, women's groups, and cultural and scientific organizations.[28] Party, Komsomol, and state officials

[25] Faizibaeva, "Novye obriady," pp. 24-25; S. Mirzoshoev, "Rasmu oinhoi nav," p. 2; "Baroi shavqei fa"olonai hayoti," *Tojikistoni Soveti*, June 14, 1985, p. 1; "Novye obriady v zhizni trudiashchikhsia," *Agitator Tadzhikistana*, 1978, no. 7 (April), pp. 36-37; Khojaev and Nu"monov, "Propagandai ateistiro," pp. 79-80.

[26] U.S. Department of State, Bureau of Intelligence and Research, "Mechanics of Nationality Politics Described by Recent Emigrés," *Soviet Nationalities Survey*, October 1-December 31, 1983, p. 6.

[27] Komilov, "Propagandai ateisti," pp. 74-75; Dadabaeva, "Sama soboi," p. 2; "Vazhnaia chast'," p. 4; "Nutqi A. Qosimov," *Tojikistoni Soveti*, January 26,1986, p. 3; "Nutqi U. Shokirov," *Tojikistoni Soveti*, January 27, 1986, p. 3; Saidbaev, *Islam i obshchestvo*, pp. 271-72; "Ateisticheskoe vospitanie trudiashchikhsia," p. 29.

[28] "Vazhnaia chast'," p. 4; "Maktab va tarbiiai ateisti khonandegon," *Gazetai muallimon*, January 14, 1984, p. 3; TadzhikTA, "Vazifahoi universitethoi khalqi," *Tojikistoni Soveti*, January 10, 1986, p. 1; Khojaev and Nu"monov, "Propagandai ateistiro," p. 77; Komilov, "Propagandai ateisti," p. 76.

from the *raion* (district) to the republican level have been criticized in recent years for insufficient effort to promote atheism.[29]

A former leader of the Communist Party of Tajikistan used one of the stock critical expressions when he complained of "serious problems" in atheist work to a 1983 party plenum. His successor echoed this complaint in 1986, but broadened it to include the republic's propaganda efforts as a whole, not just those directed against religion.[30] Soviet complaints about the quantity and quality of atheist work in Tajikistan are also found in general discussions of Islam in the Soviet Union. These shortcomings have become a scapegoat for religion's continued strength in the country.[31]

Lectures on atheism tend to be hackneyed repetitions about the harmfulness of religion. Although Tajikistan has some nine hundred atheist lecturers, few are knowledgeable about either religion or atheism.[32] Part of their problem may have to do with the lack of didactic material on atheism in the Tajik language. A textbook published in 1970 is by now outdated. Tajikistan's two main publishing houses, Donish and Irfon, published few books in the early 1980s, originals or translations, about either atheism or religion. In 1982, Irfon published none at all.[33] Literature and the arts rarely touch the issue. Few plays or films deal with the persistence of religion, and those that do tend to be superficial, poorly crafted, and so formulaic that they are barely distinguishable from each other and cannot readily attract audiences. [34]

For all the emphasis given new secular rites in the campaign against religion, these have not become well established among Soviet Muslims. The Women's Council of Tajikistan conceded that various secular rites have a negligible following in the villages.[35] Saidbaev is unusually forthright in his critique of the new rites. Those pertaining to the life cycle have no significant following, he says, in part because of the strength of people's attachment to the Islamic rites, which are deeply ingrained; and in part because of the unattractiveness of the secular, Soviet alternatives. Further, secular rites are universal in the USSR and have not been adapted to take on a local flavor; not sur-

[29] "Nutqi A. Qosimov," p. 3; TadzhikTA, "Pretvorim v zhizn'," p. 3; Kolbina, "Sviatoe mesto"; Boimurodov, "Sotsializmi mutaraqqi," p. 77; N. Safarov, "Tarbiyai ateisti," p. 2.

[30] "Kliuchevye zadachi Partiinoi organizatsii respubliki," *Agitator Tadzhikistana*, 1983, no. 16 (August), p. 10 (First Secretary R. N. Nabiev's report to the Tenth Plenum of the Central Committee of the Communist Party of Tajikistan); TadzhikTA, "Pretvorim v zhizn'," p.3.

[31] Vagabov, *Islam i voprosy*, pp. 117-19; *Islam v SSSR*, pp. 119, 131-132.

[32] "Tarbiyai ateistii mehnatkashon," *Tojikistoni Soveti*, October 19, 1985, p. 1; Madzhidov, *Osobennosti formirovaniia*, p. 56; Komilov, "Propagandai ateisti," p. 74.

[33] Jabborova, "Ba"ze problemahoi," p. 89; S. Navruzov, L. Nikolaeva, and Z. Saidov, "Maqsad: tarbiyai odami nav," *Tojikistoni Soveti*, December 3, 1985, p. 2; Rasulov and Sharifkhojaev, "Kruzhoki ta"rikh," pp. 25-26. Komilov, "Propaganda ateisti," p. 76.

[34] Ahmadov, "San"at va tashakkuli," p. 96; TadzhikTA, "Utverzhdaia pravdu zhizni," p. 2.

[35] "Baroi shavqei fa"olonai hayoti," p. 1.

prisingly, Central Asians regard them as essentially European and
therefore alien to their own heritage.[36]

The secular funeral, for example, cannot compare with the Islamic funeral as a way of expressing grief. A Komsomol wedding
involves a mass-produced ceremony at the registry office, often a trip
to a war memorial, and a certain amount of drunkenness and rowdy
behavior; no wonder young Tajiks prefer the traditional religious
ceremony.[37] Some people who feel constrained to have a Komsomol
wedding find ways to undermine its secularism. Some also go through
an Islamic ceremony. A schoolteacher from Panjikent *raion*, who is
supposed to teach atheism as part of his official duties, held a copy
of the Qur'an throughout his Komsomol wedding.[38]

A Soviet scholar admits that despite the rhetoric about the need
to instill atheism in the schools, "most of the time, atheist instruction
is the weakest part of schools' work."[39] In Dushanbe and other regions
of Tajikistan, schools commonly do little or nothing in this field for
years on end. Others do the bare minimum in a perfunctory manner.
That some teachers are themselves believers obviously weakens the
schools' contribution to antireligious efforts. Schools rarely reach students' believer parents. [40]

Atheist proselytizing, like propaganda in general, is especially
weak in rural areas both in quantity and quality. While many different
methods are supposed to be used, in practice, lectures predominate
among what little is done. Their main audience is composed of young
men, who are considered least likely to be believers. Women and
the elderly do not normally attend. Other methods to spread atheism
have fallen into disuse; little is done to spread the secular Soviet
rites.[41]

Despite the manifest deficiencies in Soviet efforts to restrict
Islam's influence, officialdom sees the survival of the religion as a less
than acute problem. Believers meet their civic responsibilities and
do not challenge the fundamental authority of the party or state. For
the present, at least, the authorities have not escalated antireligious
measures lest they drive Muslims into active opposition. The measures
used to promote atheism are so limited and ineffectual in the coun-

---

[36] Saidbaev, *Islam i obshchestvo*, pp. 229, 234-35, 274-75.
[37] N. Asadulloev, "Soiuz dvukh serdets," *Komsomolets Tadzhikistana*, July 4, 1984, p. 2.
[38] Saidbaev, *Islam i obshchestvo*, p. 256; Baimuradov, "Byt' ubezhdennym," p. 21.
[39] Jabborova, "Ba"ze problemahoi," p. 88.
[40] "Maktab va tarbiyai ateisti khonandagon," *Gazetai muallimon*, January 14, 1984, p.
3; "Maktab va tarbiyai ateisti khonandagon," *Gazetai muallimon*, January 17, 1984, p. 4;
"Maktab — tarbiyatgohi odami nav," *Gazetai muallimon*, September 6, 1983, p. 2; "Maqsadi
tarbiya — tashakkuli odami nav," *Gazetai muallimon*, September 10, 1983, p. 2; Dadabaeva,
"Konkretno-sotsiologicheskie issledovaniia," pp. 252, 257.
[41] Dadabaeva, "Konkretno-sotsiologicheskie issledovaniia," pp. 258-59; N. Safarov, "Tarbiyai ateisti," p. 2; Jabborova, "Ba"ze problemahoi," p. 89; Dzhurakulov, "Ateizmu — nastupatel'nost'," p. 26.

tryside, where most Central Asian Muslims live, that they have the unintended effect of reducing the potential for antagonizing believers.

Continuity and Revival in Soviet Islam

It is easier to demonstrate that Islam remains influential among the traditionally Muslim peoples of the Soviet Union than to determine whether its influence has increased recently in reaction to events in Iran and Afghanistan. Recent Soviet statements portray Islam as on the rise in Central Asia.[1] Outside observers must rely heavily on Soviet sources for information, but the interpretation of those sources is problematic. Criticism of party members' inaction in the face of an Islamic revival may have less to do with the status of Islam than with political disputes within the party. Or Soviet authorities may perceive Islam as stronger because they now pay it more attention. And, when all is said, the increased attention to domestic Islam has not changed in *substance* from the period before the international upsurge in Islamic activism and is still modest compared with Soviet concern about other subjects.

Soviet Islam since World War II

The Re-emergence of Islam During World War II. Islam enjoyed a certain latitude during much of the 1920s, not because the Soviet regime wished this, but because it lacked the strength to impose atheism. Starting around 1928 and lasting until World War II, Soviet policy was aggressively anti-religious. Stalin's campaigns against religion coincided with the horrors of the forced collectivization of agriculture and the terror (from the late 1920s to the late 1930s). In that exceptionally repressive climate Muslims had to be as secretive as possible about their private convictions. The crucial turning point in the status of Soviet Islam occurred after the Nazi attack on the Soviet Union when, in an effort to mobilize all available support for the war effort, Stalin granted more leeway to Russian Orthodoxy, Islam, and some other religions. Although Soviet writers sometimes treat this as a period in which adherence to Islam increased,[2] all that

---

[1] M. Mirrahimov, "Tarbiyai ateisti — vazifai muhim," *Tojikistoni Soveti*, February 11, 1986, p. 2; Jabborova, "Ba"ze problemahoi," p. 87; "Nutqi Gh. N. Qalandarov," *Tojikistoni Soveti*, January 28, 1986, p. 2.

[2] Saidbaev, *Islam i obshchestvo*, 2nd ed., p. 191.

can be said with certainty is that the display of Islamic devotion became more open, for there is no proof that religious belief had declined before the war.

Nonetheless, some Soviet specialists on Islam contend that the war stimulated greater observance, noting that those who remained at home (especially women) resorted to folk Islam to foretell the fate of their relatives serving in the military and to invoke supernatural aid to ensure their safety.[3] This suggests an analogy with Muslim behavior today with respect to the war in Afghanistan. Perhaps some of the Islamic observance that now disquiets authorities reflects the attempts of Tajikistani women to protect loved ones in a war zone with the aid of folk Islam.

Islam in the Context of Intraparty Politics. Some of the official rhetoric about the strength of Islam within the Soviet Union is not really about Islam per se, but rather about the authorities' displeasure with an official or party committee. For example, in 1985 the then-first secretary of the Communist Party of Tajikistan, R. N. Nabiev, criticized the Leninobod *oblast'* party committee for inadequate atheist propaganda in the face of a religious revival there. Religion as such may really have been his concern, but it is possible that this issue was just another charge to level against the *oblast'* committee (*obkom*) when it was the target of a barrage of criticism on a host of issues. The Central Committee of the CPSU set the stage by criticizing the *obkom* at the June 1983 plenum. Complaints included economic problems, drunkenness, weak ideological indoctrination, inadequate law enforcement, poor personnel policies, and weak Komsomol and union performance in instilling the proper attitude toward work. Thus the issue of Islamic revival in the *oblast'* was but one small item on a long list of complaints.[4]

Increased Attention and Perceptions of the Level of Religiosity. The political strength that Islam has demonstrated outside the Soviet Union since the late 1970s increased Soviet attention to an unexpected phenomenon.[5] The same applies to various Western countries as well, where there are no large domestic Muslim communities to heighten concern about the rise of Islamic activism. In itself, this attention is not proof that Islam has become more of a force within the Soviet Union. Alexandre Bennigsen's caution regarding Sufism in the Soviet Union applies equally well to Soviet Islam in general: "It is unclear at this stage whether Sufi activity is greater or simply

[3] A. Safarov, *Boqimondahoi*, p. 15; Madzhidov, *Osobennosti formirovaniia*, pp. 54-55.

[4] TadzhikTA, "Mas"uliyati olii Kommuniston," *Tojikistoni Soveti*, March 24, 1985, p. 1; "Nutqi rafiq R. N. Nabiev," ibid., April 19, 1985, pp. 1-2; "Tartibotu intizomro mustahkam kunem!" in ibid., April 19, 1985, pp. 1-3.

[5] Atkin, "Shi'ism and Social Protest," pp. 278-83; idem., "The Kremlin and Khomeini," *Washington Quarterly*, Spring 1981, pp. 54-57.

Soviet official attention to it greater than was the case before recent events in Iran and Afghanistan."[6]

Greater attention has increased the extent and changed the nature of what is noticed. The 1983 complaint of a Tajikistan official responsible for atheist propaganda points to this: he noted that the republic's Academy of Sciences had tens of specialists on atheism but that few of them visited the countryside to learn about the degree of religiosity in a given locale.[7] Heeding this and other admonishments, specialists may have now found out the situation on the ground. If so, the information that reached them and the political authorities may have come as an unpleasant surprise without necessarily reflecting a change in the nature of popular beliefs.

Charges of weak atheist proselytizing have received prominent attention in Tajikistan's Qurghonteppa *oblast'* on the border with Afghanistan. Sometime before 1984, the Tajikistan Academy of Sciences conducted a study of attitudes toward religion and atheism there (and in parts of Dushanbe), and the results may have worried officials simply because this was the kind of detailed information they had not had before. However, when First Secretary Nabiev criticized the Qurghonteppa *obkom* for numerous shortcomings in April 1985, he apparently did not consider laxity in anti-religious efforts important enough to mention.[8]

Will Muslims Challenge the USSR?

Concern About Islam's Strength Before 1979. Soviet expressions of concern about the revival of Islam since 1979 seem less portentous when compared with virtually identical statements made before then. Each time Soviet authorities directed their attention to the persistence of religion in general and Islam in particular during the 1960s and 1970s, they found the situation worrisome. They saw a revival in activity by mullahs and Sufi *ishans* in the early 1960s and remarked on the continuing strength of Islam.[9] The mullahs were alleged to be particularly active in the *oblasts* of Qurghonteppa, Kulob, and Leninobod in 1963 — just as in the 1980s.[10] Complaints about the popularity of pilgrimages to holy places could be heard then, as now.[11]

[6] Bennigsen, "Soviet Islam," p. 73.

[7] Komilov, "Propaganda ateisti," p. 75. Komilov is the special editor for atheist literature at Irfon Publishers.

[8] "Nutqi A. Qosimov," p. 4; Madzhidov, "Vospityvat' ubezhdennykh ateistov," p. 26; "Nutqi rafiq R. N. Nabiev dar plenumi komiteti partiyavii viloyati Qurghonteppa," *Tojikistoni Soveti*, April 10, 1985, pp. 1-2.

[9] A. Safarov, *Boqimondahoi*, p. 17; Kalandarov, "Rasplata za bespechnost'," p. 2; M. Khalmukhamedov, "O chem govoriat," p. 57.

[10] "Perednii krai bor'by za kommunizm," *Kommunist Tadzhikistana*, July 10, 1963, p. 1 (First Secretary D. R. Rasulov's report to the Eighth Plenum of the Central Committee of the Communist Party of Tajikistan).

[11] Surkov, "Komandirovka v rai," p. 4; Kalandarov, "Rasplata za bespechnost'," p. 2; Madzhidov, "Znachenie kul'turnoi revoliutsii," p. 37.

Then too, capitalist countries were accused of encouraging religious observance to weaken the Soviet Union.[12] And the same charge was made against Muslim countries neighboring the Soviet Union in 1965, when none of their governments supported militant Islamic movements.

Every day from Turkey, Iran, Pakistan and other countries bordering the Soviet Union every sort of nonsense from the Qur'an ... is heard by radio, including ... for the Muslims of Central Asia and Kazakhstan. They lead the religious to believe in the delights of "that world"; they call on them to stop struggling for better material conditions in earthly life and to observe strictly all the rules of dogma and ceremonies of the Islamic religion.[13]

Weak atheist propaganda and a permissive attitude toward religion by the party, mass media, and the schools were blamed for the spread of religious observance.[14]

Party policy for the Soviet Union as a whole repeatedly demanded vigorous efforts to spread atheism in the 1960s and 1970s. The best known of these was Khrushchev's crude anti-religions campaign in 1959-1964. Again in 1971, the Central Committee of the CPSU called for more atheist work and more strict enforcement of Soviet law regarding religion. In 1976, the Twenty-Fifth Congress of the CPSU expressed a similar view.[15]

Anti-religious measures in Tajikistan also pre-date 1979. A call to supplant religious holidays with Soviet holidays went out in 1972, just as in 1983.[16] Tajikistan's House of Scientific Atheism, the coordinator of research and methodological work on atheism, opened in 1972.[17] Special history courses on atheism at Tajikistan State University date from the 1968-69 academic year.[18] Courses to teach atheism to women and the general populace date from 1962 and 1976.[19] Lectures on atheism increased rapidly in number between 1971 and 1978.[20]

Post-1979 Propaganda. Although Soviet rhetoric about Islam has increased since 1979,[21] the subject is still only one of many addressed by Soviet propaganda; further, it still ranks far behind economic

---

[12] A. Safarov, *Boqimondahoi*, pp. 15-16; Madzhidov, *Osobennosti formirovaniia*, p. 54; A. Andronov, "Neprimirimost' k perezhitkam," *Agitator Tadzhikistana*, 1977, no. 2 (January), p. 15.

[13] A. Safarov, *Boqimondahoi*, p. 16.

[14] Ibid., pp. 16-17, 36-37; Kalandarov, "Rasplata za bespechnost'," p. 2; "Perednii krai bor'by," pp. 1-2; "Komandirovka v rai zakonchilos," *Izvestiia*, January 23, 1964, p. 4.; Khashimov, "Religiia i byt," pp. 66-67; *Agitator Tadzhikistana*, 1978, no. 6 (March), pp. 24-26 ; "Ob usilenii ateisticheskogo vospitaniia naseleniia," *Ob ideologicheskoi rabote KPSS* (Moscow: Politizdat, 1977), pp. 309-10.

[15] "Ob usilenii," pp. 309-10; Baimurodov, *Leninskii printsip*, p. 83.

[16] U. Sharifov, "Dasturi mufid," *Tojikistoni Soveti*, July 10, 1985, p. 3.

[17] *Islam v SSSR*, p. 142.

[18] Ibid., p. 141.

[19] Vagabov, *Islam i voprosy*, p. 147; "Ateisticheskoe vospitanie trudiashchikhsia," p. 28.

[20] Baimurodov, *Leninskii printsip*, p. 94.

[21] In particular, there was a spurt of publications especially in 1980 and 1981. A. Bennigsen, "Soviet Islam," p. 65.

concerns or the general state of U.S.-Soviet relations. The June 1983 Plenum of the Central Committee of the CPSU focused on ideological and propaganda issues. Konstantin Chernenko's address called for efforts to weaken the influence of religion. At the same time, he discussed at greater length the importance of propaganda to combat economic problems, alcoholism, hooliganism, and having no visible means of support; to teach the ideas of Marx, Engels, and Lenin; and to extol the achievements of the Soviet Union.[22] A 1985 list of counter-propaganda topics for Tajikistan reflects the distribution of attention in the mass media in general. Only a few topics refer, directly or indirectly, to religion:

The irreconcilability of bourgeois and communist ideologies. The basic orientation of the ideological struggle and counterpropaganda. Counter-propaganda as part of the work of party organizations. Fictions of bourgeois and reformist propaganda about socialist democracy, the rights of Soviet citizens. The suppression of civil liberties in the United States. Unemployment, inflation, crime always accompany capitalism. Two worlds, two ways of life. Evidence of the strength of the Soviet system. Tajikistan as seen by anti-Communists. Main themes of bourgeois propaganda aimed at Soviet youth. The USIA (United States Information Agency). Freedom of conscience in the Soviet Union and anti-Communist propaganda. Imperialist propaganda about nationalism in the Soviet Union. The ideological expansion of imperialism and the necessity of increased political vigilance. Distortions by anti-communist propaganda about the role of the CPSU in Soviet politics. Education in the Soviet Union and the West. Social security in the Soviet Union and the West.[23]

Agitator Tadzhikistana, the journal aimed at those engaged in mass propaganda, devoted about a half-dozen articles per year in the 1979-1985 period to religious issues in general, Islam, Christianity and techniques of atheist propaganda — and this in a journal that prints nearly 300 articles a year.[24]

Many catchwords of Soviet propaganda that seem to be veiled references to religion can also refer to matters far removed. "Unethical" or "immoral" behavior, "survivals of the past" (*perezhitki*) and an "un-Soviet way of life" may refer to hooliganism, drunkenness, having no visible means of support, bad attitudes toward work, or a craving for consumer goods as well as to religious observance.[25]

Not only does combating religion receive less attention than economic and other issues, but there are also times when the subject is conspicuously absent. Leonid Brezhnev's report to the Twenty-Sixth Congress of the CPSU in 1981 dealt with molding the right political and ideological attitudes, the usual context for mentioning

[22] "Aktual'nye voprosy ideologicheskoi, massovo-politicheskoi raboty," pp. 15-18, 24.

[23] "Premernaia tematika," *Agitator Tadzhikistana*, 1985, no. 5 (March), p. 20.

[24] The survey is only approximate, because it was not possible to obtain every issue for each of the years in question. For every year except 1983, nineteen or more issues were consulted, for 1983, only thirteen.

[25] R. Taghoeva, "Kompleksi va muttasilii kori ideaviyu tarbiyavi," *Kommunisti Tojikiston*, 1985, no. 2 (February) p. 75; Andronov, "Neprimirimost' k perezhitkam," p. 15; "Rezoliutsiia XIX s"ezda Kommunisticheskoi partii Tadzhikistana," *Agitator Tadzhikistana*, 1981, no. 5 (March), p. 15; *Materialy XXV s"ezda KPSS* (Moscow: Politizdat, 1976), p. 78.

religion and atheism, but he did not discuss either.[26] The speech of Tajikistan's chief prosecutor, Iu. N. Shcherbakov, to the Twentieth Congress of the Communist Party of Tajikistan in 1986 did not call for stricter enforcement of the law on religious organizations.[27] For all the concern expressed about the susceptibility of the young to Islam, two of the most important recent discussions of propaganda objectives among young Tajikistanis ignored the religious issue.[28]

Sometimes the official assessment of Islam's challenge changes so suddenly as to raise doubts about how much the status of Islam is really the issue. For example, atheist work in the southern *oblast's*, Qurghonteppa and Kulob, received positive coverage in 1983, and religion was not portrayed as a problem. In 1985, when both *oblast's* came under criticism for a variety of failings, inaction in the face of religious persistence was not counted among them. Then, at the Twentieth Congress of Tajikistan's party in January 1986, First Secretary Mahkamov singled out the two *oblast's* as places where religious observance had hardly declined.[29] An outside observer is inclined to suspect that issues other than the status of Islam motivated Mahkamov's criticism.

Prospects for an Islamic Challenge to Soviet Hegemony in Tajikistan. Some Western observers have associated recent violent outbursts in Central Asia with a new Islamic militancy which may in the long run threaten Soviet political authority. But the evidence does not support such an association. The most serious outburst of opposition in Central Asia since World War II was the Tashkent riot of 1969. While there is no specific information on the motives or ideology of the instigators, Islam probably was not a crucial factor; the instigators apparently were male students at Uzbekistan's institutions of higher education, one of the social elements considered least likely to remain religious. Their placards displayed anti-Soviet and anti-Russian messages, not Islamic ones.[30]

Moreover, inspiration by Islamic political militance abroad could not have contributed to the outburst because such militance was not

[26] "Otchet Tsentral'nogo Komiteta KPSS XXVI s"ezdu Kommunisticheskoi Partii Sovetskogo Soiuza i ocherednye zadachi partii v oblasti vnutrennei i vneshnei politiki," *Ob ideologicheskoi rabote KPSS*, 2nd rev. ed. (Moscow: Politizdat, 1983), pp. 50-123.

[27] "Nutqi Iu. N. Shcherbakov," *Tojikistoni Soveti*, January 27, 1986, p. 4.

[28] TadzhikTA, "Kuvvai Komsomol dar rohbarii partiyaviist," *Tojikistoni Soveti*, January 6, 1985, p. 1 (a report of the Twelfth Plenum of the Central Committee of the Communist Party of Tajikistan); O. B. Karimova (director of the Tajikistan State Institute of Scientific Research in Pedagogy), "Dar javonon parvaridani shuurnokii siyosi va oshtinopaziri nisbat ba ideologiyayu akhloqi bourzhuazi," *Maktabi Soveti*, 1985, no. 10 (October), pp. 15-19.

[29] *Kommunist Tadzhikistana*, January 26, 1986, p. 3; Tagaeva, "Doiti do serdtsa kazhdogo," p. 22 (R. Taghoeva [Tagaeva] is a secretary of the Kulob *obkom*); R. Ahmedova (a secretary of the Qurghonteppa obkom), "Na osnove kompleksnogo podkhoda," *Agitator Tadzhikistana*, 1983, no. 23 (December), pp. 15-16; "Nutqi rafiq R. N. Nabiev dar plenumi komiteti partiyavii viloyati Qurghonteppa," *Tojikistoni Soveti*, April 10, 1985, pp. 1-2; M. Qosimov, "Az mavqei sertalabi," *Tojikistoni Soveti*, December 14, 1985, p. 3.

[30] U.S. Department of State, "Mechanics of Nationality Politics," pp. 6-7.

then a powerful force in the Islamic world. Instead, nationalism, modernization, conservatism, and Islamic or nationalist varieties of socialism were all far more influential in Islamic countries. At that time, Afghanistan was ruled by a monarchy that followed a program of limited and somewhat ineffective modernizing reforms and maintained a good working relationship with the Soviet Union. What opposition there was to the Kabul regime came from those who wanted more change (whether in the form of modernizing reforms or socialism), not from Islam, which was not under pressure. In Iran, the monarchy continued the reforms of the "White Revolution" and appeared to have triumphed over the militant Islamic opposition, led by Ayatollah Khomeini, who seemed to have entered political oblivion when he was exiled in 1964. Soviet-Iranian relations improved during the 1960s.

According to a Chinese source, there was another outburst of violence, an "ethnic clash" in Dushanbe, in September 1978.[31] The nature of the source makes it difficult to ascertain what really happened, because China's purpose in reporting the story was to attack the "revisionist renegade clique" in the Kremlin for "oppressing the various nationalities," not to analyze the dynamics of Tajikistani politics.[32] The account provides no information on the causes of the disturbance or on who was involved, but according to the story from Beijing, the grievance was cast in ethnic, not religious, terms. In any event, foreign religious inspiration is unlikely in this case, too. By September 1978 the Islamic opposition in Iran had demonstrated considerable strength, but the government's use of force against it had also intensified and the outcome of the power struggle remained uncertain. In Afghanistan, opponents of the new communist regime had not yet launched widespread hostilities in the name of Islam; that began later in the year.

A disturbance related directly to Islamic activism in Tajikistan did occur in the provincial capital of Qurghonteppa in August 1986. As described above (in Chapter Two), a Wahhabi mullah, Abdullo Saidov, was arrested on charges of slandering the Soviet state and society after he called for the creation of an Islamic state in Tajikistan. His kinsmen organized a demonstration at the city's office of the Ministry of Internal Affairs to demand his release. Present in addition to his relatives were some neighbors from the *sovkhoz* (state farm) where he lived, some of his followers, and miscellaneous townsmen not clearly identified in the press accounts. Heated words were spoken but there was no violence. The confrontation ended without escalating into a major incident. Saidov and his followers were sentenced to prison terms. Two officials of his *sovkhoz* were disciplined

---

[31] "Ethnic Conflict," *Beijing Review*, January 5, 1979, p. 27.
[32] Ibid.

for turning a blind eye to his activities. The first secretary of the Vakhsh *raion* party committee, A. Khudoidodov, was severely reprimanded by the party for the same reason.[33] This was a warning to officials to nip in the bud any manifestations of Islamic militancy. Subsequently, the KGB chief in Tajikistan, V. V. Petkel', revealed that "dozens" of trails of unofficial mullahs took place in 1986 and 1987. He stated that they not only stimulated religion but also urged an anti-Soviet jihad.[34]

In December 1986 there were two days of student riots in Alma-Ata, the capital of Kazakhstan, in reaction to the ouster of a Kazakh as first secretary of the republic's party organization and his replacement by a Russian. Even though Russians constitute the single largest nationality in Kazakhstan, this change was an extraordinarily impolitic move by Moscow. Since 1983 all the other republican first secretaries in Central Asia have been replaced. (The Uzbek party chief died in office; those in Tajikistan, Turkmenistan, and Kirghizia were removed.) In each case the new first secretary belonged to the republic's titular nationality. By departing from this practice in the Kazakhstan change, Moscow cast doubt on the informal affirmative-action policy that has given non-Russians access to certain kinds of jobs. Therefore it is not surprising that urban Kazakh students, who would expect to benefit from such a policy, responded angrily to the leadership change. One need not look to Islamic militancy to explain the student riots. Because pejoratives like "hooligans" and "parasites" are stock insults used in official Soviet reports, they reveal nothing about the instigators of the riots.

Ultimately, it should be kept in mind that all these incidents were isolated events and that the Soviet authorities demonstrated the willingness and ability to use force to stop any open demonstration of unrest. It should also be remembered that stories of Islamic unrest in Soviet Central Asia spread by expatriot groups in the West are not always reliable. When Mikhail Gorbachev came to Washington in December 1987, one of many groups marching in protest carried a banner reading "Free Turkestan" but that does not mean that anything of significance is happening in Turkestan, or that there was any connection between a putative "movement" in Turkestan and those marching in Washington.[35] Doris Lessing apparently believed a tale told her by an Afghan *mujahid* that the Turkomans have been fighting the Russians for seventy years, but no one else has to believe it.[36]

---

[33] Sanginov, "Ashki nadomat," p. 4; Rabiev, "V klass . . . s koranom?" p. 2; idem, "Iduschchie v nikuda," p. 3.

[34] Foreign Broadcast Information Service, *Soviet Union. Daily Report*, January 11, 1988, p. 58.

[35] *The New York Times*, December 8, 1987.

[36] D. Lessing, *The Wind Blows Away Our Words: A First Hand Account of the Afghan Resistance* (New York: Vintage, 1987), p. 91.

Soviet media normally portray issues in polar extremes. Things are wonderful or terrible, or both simultaneously; there is no middle ground. On the positive side, they paint a picture of highly motivated patriots committed to socialist ideals performing their duties admirably; economic objectives met or exceeded; the widespread and vigorous implementation of party policies. On the negative side, there are "shortcomings" and sometimes even "serious shortcomings," code words for a recognition that everything works poorly. Failings are discussed with tones of indignation and concern. The authorities' solution lies partially in policy changes but relies heavily on exhorting the public to be zealous builders of communism. There seems to be a faith in the value of correct exhortation. Thus, calls for more and better propaganda are a prominent part of the approach to most major issues.

The post-1979 rhetoric about Islam's strength in the Soviet Union fits within this framework. It is nothing new or different; it certainly does not prove that there has been a change in the nature of Soviet Muslims' religiosity or in state attitudes toward Islam.

Prospects for Islam in Tajikistan

Islam in Tajikistan has retained a broad following throughout the Soviet era. Despite constraints and periods of persecution, Islamic life continues much as it does in most Muslim countries: believers still meet many of the formal and informal obligations of establishment Islam and also look to folk Islam for help in a host of areas. For both Muslims who practice and many of those who do not, Islam remains an integral part of their ethnic identity and way of life.

All this was true before the international wave of Islamic political activism in the 1970s. That upsurge may have influenced the Muslims of Tajikistan but such influence need not lead to political radicalization. It could take the form of increased pride in one's Islamic heritage or greater interest in Islam's ethical and spiritual values; any political ramifications of such developments would be modest. Even if whatever influence may be exerted affects political attitudes, that does not necessitate that a substantial political movement will result. The decentralized structure of Soviet Islam (except for the government-controlled official administration) is ill-suited to mobilizing cohesive mass support.

There is no reliable evidence that Islamic identity in Tajikistan differs now from what it had been before the late 1970s. True, Soviet authorities have increased their attention to the persistence of Islam, but this seems part of a cycle of periodic alarms alternating with periods of decreased attention. As if to prove this, the nature of complaints about Islam has not changed. The fundamental problem is still that Islam competes with Marxism-Leninism as a system of this-worldly values and impedes the creation of a homogeneous Soviet society. To pose such an obstacle, Islam need merely preserve its traditional character rather than take on a new political militance, as it has in some Islamic states.

Religious identity coexists in each individual believer with other kinds of identity, including nationality, age, occupation, institutional affiliation, sex, class, and education. Which allegiance matters most at a given time depends on circumstance.[1] Moreover, a strong sense of religious or national identity does not automaticaly evoke a strong sense of discontent along those lines. This is particularly likely to be the case in Tajikistan and other Central Asian republics where the concentration of the Muslim nationalities in the countryside makes them relatively less subject to the urban-based regulatory powers. This inadvertently allows the indigenous nationalities more leeway to preserve their religious and ethnic traditions. Even where religious or ethnic discontent does exist, it need not always produce political opposition movements that go so far as to challenge the regime's authority. Personal, private resistance need not add up to a significant social force. Political discontent exists in many countries but attempts to overthrow a government because of that are the exception, not the rule. That applies particularly to the Soviet Union, where the leadership has so amply demonstrated to the citizens that it is ready to crush all real or imagined opposition. Furthermore, the Soviet leadership uses a variety of measures apart from force to co-opt minorities. It also allows some latitude in areas like religion, where the costs of a complete victory could be counterproductively high.

Geoffrey Wheeler's 1968 assessment of Islam's influence in Central Asia rings as true today as it did then:

Islam undoubtedly constitutes some sort of bond of union among the Soviet Muslim nationalities, and also between them and non-Soviet Muslims. But this does not necessarily mean that there is such a thing as Muslim nationalism or Turkic nationalism or Turkestani nationalism.[2]

Thus the existence of Islam in the Soviet Union is an obstacle to the creation of a homogeneous society. It is likely a factor in some Soviet foreign-policy decisions, although probably a minor one. Soviet rule, in turn, sets parameters on the kinds of expression Islam can take in Tajikistan and all of Soviet Central Asia. The Soviet system cannot destroy religion or the religious elements within national cultures in Central Asia, but it can squelch virtually any and all political dissent that may derive from them. Thus, neither the disappearance of Islam nor the disappearance of Soviet rule in Central Asia is a likely prospect.

---

[1] G. W. Lapidus, "Ethnonationalism and Political Stability: The Soviet Case," *World Politics*, July 1984, pp. 560-62, 577.

[2] G. Wheeler, "National and Religious Consciousness in Soviet Islam," *Survey*, January 1968, p. 74.

FOREIGN POLICY RESEARCH INSTITUTE

Founded in 1955, the Foreign Policy Research Institute is an independent, publicly supported, nonprofit organization devoted to the public dissemination of scholarly research affecting the national interests of the United States. As a catalyst for the exchange of ideas, FPRI seeks to shape the climate in which American foreign policy is made. Research is conducted by the FPRI's staff, supplemented by the work of Fellows and Associate Scholars.

In addition to *The Philadelphia Papers,* the Foreign Policy Research Institute publishes ORBIS, a quarterly journal of world affairs. The *FPRI Book Series* includes volumes on the cutting edge of research.

FPRI administers the *Inter-University Seminar on Foreign Affairs,* which regularly brings together scholars and businessmen for lectures, seminars, and workshops on international issues. Each year the Institute sponsors a competition for the *Thornton D. Hooper Fellowship in International Affairs;* the Hooper Fellow spends a year in residence at FPRI conducting independent research. The FPRI *Internship Program* provides opportunities for students who are contemplating a career in international affairs.

All contributions to the Institute are tax-deductible.

Editors: ADAM M. GARFINKLE and DANIEL PIPES
Managing Editor: ROGER S. DONWAY
Manuscript Editor: JOANN TOMAZINIS
Assistant Editor: MARK W. POWELL

BOARD OF EDITORS

BACK TITLES IN PRINT

Adam M. Garfinkle, **The Politics of the Nuclear Freeze,** 1984. 258 pp. $7.95.

Colin S. Gray, **Nuclear Strategy and Strategic Planning,** 1984. 130 pp. $5.95.

Robert F. Turner, **The War Powers Resolution: Its Implementation in Theory and Practice,** with a foreword by Senator John Tower, 1983. 147 pp. $4.95.

Shaheen Ayubi, Richard Bissell, et al., **Economic Sanctions in U.S. Foreign Policy, 1982.** 86 pp. $3.95.

Staff of the Foreign Policy Research Institute, **The Three Percent Solution and the Future of NATO,** 1981. 118 pp. $6.96.

Harvey Sicherman, **Broker or Advocate: The U.S. Role in the Arab-Israeli Dispute, 1973-1978,** 1979. 120 pp. $5.95.

Nimrod Novik, **On the Shores of Bab al-Mandeb: Soviet Diplomacy and Regional Dynamics,** 1979. 83 pp. $3.95.

Adam M. Garfinkle, **"Finlandization": A Map to a Metaphor,** 1978. 56 pp. $3.95.